The
ADD and ADHD
Cure

The
ADD and ADHD
Cure

The Natural Way to Treat Hyperactivity and Refocus Your Child

JAY GORDON, MD

with Jennifer Chang

WILEY

John Wiley & Sons, Inc.

Published by John Wiley & Sons, Inc., Hoboken, New Jersey
Published simultaneously in Canada

The information contained in this book is not intended to serve as a replacement for professional medical advice. Any use of the information in this book is at the reader's discretion. The author and the publisher specifically disclaim any and all liability arising directly or indirectly from the use or application of any information contained in this book. A health care professional should be consulted regarding your specific situation.

For general information about our other products and services, please contact our Customer Care Department within the United States at (800) 762-2974, outside the United States at (317) 572-3993 or fax (317) 572-4002.

Wiley also publishes its books in a variety of electronic formats. Some content that appears in print may not be available in electronic books. For more information about Wiley products, visit our web site at www.wiley.com.

Library of Congress Cataloging-in-Publication Data:

Gordon, Jay, date.
   The ADD and ADHD cure : the natural way to treat hyperactivity and refocus your child / Jay Gordon.
      p. cm.
   Includes bibliographical references and index.
   ISBN 978-0-470-07268-4 (cloth)
   1. Attention-deficit hyperactivity disorder—Popular works. I. Title.
   RJ506.H9G666 2008
   618.92'8589—dc22

                                                    2008022133

Printed in the United States of America

10 9 8 7 6 5 4 3 2 1

CONTENTS

ACKNOWLEDGMENTS

I have always wanted to write a book that says as plainly as possible, "Change the way you eat and you can change the way you feel and behave." This concept is even more crucial as we raise our children.

Thanks to Christel Winkler at John Wiley & Sons for understanding that a doctor/author with ADD who is writing a book about ADD and ADHD was probably going to deliver chapters and revisions late. Often quite late.

Mari Florence and Skye Van Raalte-Herzog put this project together. Thank you.

Jennifer Chang's name is on the cover of this book with mine because, while I might have had some good ideas about treating ADD/ADHD naturally, she had the natural writing skills. Great job, Jennifer!

My wife, Meyera Robbins, created the recipes, cooking ideas, and meal plans, as well as edited the manuscript with me, and should have her name on the cover, too, above mine. She deserves all the credit when your children and family love the meals and snacks presented in this book. Anything I ever write is dedicated to Meyera. If you think coping with your child's attention deficit is difficult, you should try switching places with my wife as she copes with my (unmedicated) ADD year after year.

Our daughter, Simone, gets credit for inspiring me and being the greatest kid ever.

Thanks to a real professional author, Seth Greenland, for telling me that an overly effusive acknowledgments page is not needed. I thank you effusively for that advice and will now list just a few more people who helped get me through the day and a few more who agreed to look at the finished book and perhaps lend their names and good wishes to the back cover.

Thanks to Cheryl Taylor, who has run my Web site, www.drjay gordon.com, for years and has helped thousands of parents navigate the early weeks and months of their babies' lives.

I have worked with an incredible office staff for nearly twenty years. Ileana, Lisa, Marci, Beverly, Jennifer, Holly, Lex, Sophia, Ranessa, and the rest of my team keep me as organized as they possibly can. Sometimes it works, sometimes it doesn't. My medical partners, Linda Nussbaum and Jody Lappin, deserve thanks for giving me a little extra time to work on this book.

Thanks, Tobey and Jen, Noah and Tracy, Ben and Laura, Julia and Danny, Casey and Summer, Mariska and Peter, John McD Edison, Matt and Lucy, Courteney and David, Carrie-Anne and Steven, Arianna, Brooke, Cindy and Randy, and David and Tea. These very successful friends of mine may or may not have the elements of adult ADD, but they sure are accomplished multitaskers, and I won't pry by asking their parents how much fun they were as kids. I thank them all for agreeing to look at the final draft and perhaps add a little luster to the book's cover.

I receive phone calls and e-mail messages almost every day from parents whose kids with ADD/ADHD have worked hard and succeeded in school and life using the techniques I've outlined here. I have always maintained that successful adult multitasking flows quite organically from well-cared-for children and teenagers with ADD and ADHD. Try it!

Introduction

If you've picked up this book, your family (or a family close to you) is dealing with a child's attention deficit disorder (ADD) or the hyperactive variation (ADHD). Perhaps it was just a nagging feeling that something was not right or maybe your child's school suggested something that sent you to the bookstore. It doesn't matter how you got here; you're in the right place now.

The ADD and ADHD Cure isn't a reference guide on what ADD/ADHD is or is not, and this book doesn't provide you with the diagnostic tools for determining whether your child has either condition. (If you suspect that your child does have ADD/ADHD, you should schedule an appointment with his or her pediatrician.) What this book does do is provide a safe and effective nondrug protocol that has been used in my practice for over twenty-five years to successfully treat thousands of children and restore their quality of life.

I'm going to give away the ending of the book now, even before you begin reading it: We can do better!

The many children who are being misdiagnosed with behavioral syndromes can be and *are* helped with relatively simple changes in diet and lifestyle. The "epidemic" of behavioral disorders in the United States today is supposedly being "cured" by pharmaceuticals. Often we don't even know what is wrong, but we know that there is a drug for it. This is what usually happens with ADD/ADHD. Families are so concerned that their child will suffer academically, emotionally, or socially from what is perceived as ADD/ADHD that they immediately head to their pediatrician or psychiatrist and agree to put their child on some very serious medication—drugs that the child will likely take until adulthood, if not beyond. This book provides a nondrug solution in the form of positive lifestyle changes, which include the following:

Eating Real Food

Michael Pollan wrote an excellent book, *In Defense of Food*, in which he tells his readers that processed foods, so-called healthy alternatives to whole foods, and supplements should be avoided. I agree completely. Feed your child a simple, elegant diet of fresh fruits, vegetables, grains, and beans whenever you can. Avoid foods with additives, because your child is better off eating the real thing. Everything we need for good mental and physical health can be found in simple meals of whole foods.

Getting Up, Getting Out, and Exercising

Exercise strongly and positively improves the way the brain and the body work. Conversely, inactivity, in the form of watching TV and playing computer games, has very negative effects on brain chemistry, fitness, and, particularly, ADD/ADHD.

Getting Enough Sleep

I have many patients who don't seem to grasp this concept. They'll say, "I'm so tired and my child's so tired, and I think we should have some blood tests to find out why." Sometimes I want to say them, "Instead of blood tests, let me X-ray your brain." We're tired and lethargic when we don't get enough sleep.

Setting Limits and Structuring Time at Home

Structuring your child's time at home can have a positive effect on his or her behavior at school. Though this sounds obvious, I am sad to say that many parents and educators don't seem to know this. Make sensible rules about behavior and limits when it comes to bedtime, computer time, exercise, or food choices. If you don't do this at home, don't expect teachers to suddenly be able to flip a switch on your kid's behavior at school. Likewise, a school that is too relaxed about rules and homework deadlines or has unrealistic demands will probably be a negative influence on your child.

I'm not going to disparage any parent's decision to put his or her child on medication. As a parent myself, and as a pediatrician who has counseled literally thousands of parents in my medical practice, I know that these decisions are not taken lightly. However, I can tell you today that the stories and articles you've read and heard about loss of appetite, a "crash" at the end of the day . . . these are all true. Medicines may lessen the symptoms of ADD/ADHD, but they don't address the underlying problems of poor diet, lack of exercise, lack of sleep, and lack of parental guidance.

I would like to introduce another option for coping with ADD/ADHD and the many symptoms that look like ADD/ADHD. If you follow my protocol, your child will improve dramatically, and many, if not most, will not need to go on medication.

Don't you think this option is worth trying?

Many of the families who visit my practice struggle with the concept of changing their child's diet and sleep schedule and adding more exercise and structure. Remind yourself that all change can be difficult. Yes, if your child has been sitting in front of a television or spending all of his or her free time playing video games, it will be hard to get your child excited by soccer. And yes, it's hard to go from take-out dinners and prepackaged meals to freshly prepared meals with no processed ingredients. But it can be done, and *the change is worth it.* Perhaps you have some trouble setting boundaries on your child's behavior. You must. Do it for your child. It's worth it.

Before you really get into reading *The ADD and ADHD Cure,* please look around your house, your refrigerator, your lives, and start right now.

Like most parents today, you're no doubt busy with work and family and probably don't have time to sit and read an entire book in one sitting—especially with a child in crisis—so that is why I chose to write the book in several sections. The first section is an overview of my protocol and gives you the basic tools to start a plan for your family. Once you're set squarely on the plan, you can read the second section for the details on managing the finer points of your child's health, and for the next major steps to take in putting your child on the road to recovery. The third and final section provides additional help, not just for your child but also for the entire family.

Why do I keep repeating the word "family"? Because my ideas involve diet and lifestyle changes, and families find the greatest success with the plan if all members band together and face the child's challenge as a cohesive unit. You'll find that it is much easier to set limits for one child when the others have the same rules. You can't feed one child healthy, nutritionally balanced meals while permitting the others to eat greasy French fries from the local drive-thru. Fairness, consistency, and a positive attitude are your best tools for successfully managing your child's condition.

Remember, it's worth it.

PART I

The Quick Start

1

The ADD and ADHD Cure

I began practicing pediatric medicine nearly thirty years ago. When I first started out, I saw an awful lot of kids who had problems that couldn't be resolved in "conventional" ways. If I treated them with medication—the norm at that time—often the side effects of the medication were worse than the original disease. This still happens today, even with newer medicines. There are dozens more new drugs in hundreds of different dosage forms, and thousands of side effects.

Over the years, public understanding of behavior disorders—particularly, attention deficit disorder (ADD) and the hyperactive variation (ADHD)—steadily grew through wider media coverage and the availability of resources on the disorder. My understanding of attention-deficit issues grew not so much from reading but from watching children get into trouble at school, lose friends, and miss out on invitations to birthday parties. This was because their particular way of thinking and interacting made them just plain difficult. Parents helped me to recognize all of these factors as the first clues pointing to the presence of ADD/ADHD in their child.

The road to diagnosis would look something like this: a parent of one of my patients would, in speaking with the child's kindergarten, first-grade, or second-grade teacher in the first week of school, discover that the child had a minor "hitting," "fidgeting," or otherwise disruptive problem. Typically, both the parent and the teacher would be somewhat dismissive about the severity of the situation. "Oh, I'm sure it'll be fine. He [She] must be having a hard time adjusting, that's all."

A week or two later, a notice might be sent home from the teacher. "You know, your child has trouble following directions and getting along with others." At this stage, many patients' parents bring the issue to my attention, and it is at this point that I urge them to consider the possibility of ADD/ADHD. I recommend immediate measures to mitigate the symptoms, and I tell the parents that if they don't do something now, it will only get worse. The child's continued disruptive behavior eventually forces the school to recommend that he or she undergo testing, and following a formal diagnosis, the child is subsequently placed in an individualized educational program. Then most parents are offered no other option than stimulant medication to control their child's ADD/ADHD. For any family, this is a difficult and disruptive decision.

In my work, I witness firsthand the detrimental effects of medication on a child's development. Everything from day-to-day moods to physical development and self-esteem are adversely affected, and oftentimes the side effects are heartbreaking to watch. When I started my career as a pediatrician, medication was understood to be the *only* option, not only for ADD/ADHD but also for most childhood ailments.

I began looking at alternative ways of treating everything from ear infections to behavioral problems. I found that there were much more logical ways than medication of helping families cope with childhood and teenage health concerns. Often, these methods worked better—and *always* had the added bonus of producing fewer side effects.

Behavioral problems are very common in pediatrics. They run the gamut from very difficult eighteen-month-old babies to oppositional eighteen-year-olds, but by far, attention deficit disorder is the most diagnosed. For my patients' families, ADD and ADHD represented a life-changing challenge that drove many worried parents to resort, unquestioningly, to drug treatment and all the accompanying side effects. Parents and families in crisis made me realize I had to help them find a way to treat ADD and ADHD without medication.

Most kids today eat a tremendous amount of sugar. They eat a lot of processed foods: foods with virtually no nutritional value but added artificial colors, artificial flavorings, and preservatives. In short, they are eating miserable, artificial, overprocessed *junk.* Government agencies do not protect the nutritional health of children, and parents and doctors have trouble standing up to the withering assault of billions of dollars spent advertising this nearly toxic diet.

Children don't get enough sleep, not enough downtime, and hardly any quiet time—and they certainly don't get enough exercise.

Homework saps time and energy, starting in the *first or second grade* (have we gone crazy?) and reaching crushing levels by middle school. I've watched lovely natural little athletes turn into stationary lumps in just a few short years because many schools do not incorporate enough physical education classes or offer enough healthy options for lunch and snacks.

The twenty-first-century lifestyle compromises the human body by forcing it to always run at half capacity (as it expends energy on processing junk through the digestive system) and consequently does ongoing harm to the physical *and* mental development of a growing child. We need to reverse this trend and treat ADD/ADHD and other behavioral issues as a medical emergency.

It seems clear to me that to begin this change, we need only to apply some simple, harmless interventions, like telling parents to try a week or two with no sugar in their child's diet—or better still, a week or two without dairy and sugar. These are things that might be viewed by some parents as extreme measures, but my response is always, "You think *that* is extreme but you don't think that ten or twenty years on Ritalin is?"

When I put it this way, many parents are willing to give my ideas a chance. And, amazingly, they discover for themselves what I already know through practice: when kids don't get an excess of sugar, they behave *very* differently. When children and teens are given a good, nutritious diet and when you arrange and enforce a schedule that allows more sleep and more structure, you discover a child who can sit and learn and take directions. The change is nothing short of remarkable, and it comes from the "sacrifice" of eating healthy foods, playing outside more, and getting a good night's sleep.

Every parent knows what happens when a kid comes home from a birthday party. In fact, I used to tell people, "If you're going to feed my daughter cookies, soda, ice cream, birthday cake, pizza, and some candy from a piñata, please keep her overnight. It's no fun to pick her up at five in the evening and deal with her in that state until bedtime."

There is a medical term for what happens to the body after a heavy intake of sugar, because the physical, emotional, and cognitive effects are very real. It's called *reactive hypoglycemia.* The high blood sugar from all this "celebration" food causes an outpouring of insulin, which then leads to very low blood sugar in reaction. Over a short time, the blood sugar plummets from its great height, and a child gets the twitchy bottom syndrome and simply can't sit still. They can be sad, angry, or sleepy. In adults, we call it the coffee-break syndrome. About an hour after you consume a coffee and a doughnut, the "high" wears off and you "need" more coffee and another doughnut. You're on a merry-go-round that is essentially a sugar-rush-and-crash cycle.

For some kids (and adults, too) the effects are so notable that what might be thought of as a normal intake of sugar during the day can interfere with study, work, and play for hours in school or anywhere else. Virtually all experts agree that ADD magnifies all the negative effects from sugar and can seriously undermine a child's educational and social life.

What's Really Going On

I'm sure that ADD and ADHD are being overdiagnosed these days. The media, medical, and pharmaceutical attention the disorders have drawn has led parents and doctors to jump to the diagnosis of ADD and ADHD almost automatically. Instead, we ought to look harder for the nutritional and behavioral issues that might cause the symptoms of ADD and ADHD.

Instead of relying on the ADD/ADHD label, we should think harder about the kids who might have done better in a different school or on a different diet, or with a little more exercise or with more limits at home, or perhaps even with just some more sleep. It's true: some kids do have unusual brain chemistry. They actually have aclinical/psychological/ psychiatric diagnosis of ADD or ADHD, established through the appropriate tests. Nevertheless, even those kids—*especially* those kids—will benefit from a better diet with much less sugar and a few lifestyle changes.

Although there is not agreement in the pediatric literature about sugar and ADD/ADHD, any parent—or any pediatrician and, certainly, any teacher—will tell you what happens to children on cupcake days at school. So why do we continue feeding a child with behavioral problems the very things that are known to cause and exacerbate these problems in *all* children?

As parents and caregivers, *we need to believe our eyes.* There might be plenty of books and articles that say sugar doesn't have an impact on behavior, and they're simply absurd. It's even been recognized in a court of law that if you eat enough junk food it can lead to serious misbehavior.

In the earlier years of my career, I'm sorry to say, I was too dismissive of disruptive behavior in children. I'd say, "Oh, he's three or four years old and the school has to lighten up—they have to understand that's how children that age behave." I now know that kind of dismissive attitude does a disservice to the child and to the whole family, because, in fact, schools have seen hundreds and hundreds of kids over the years. When a school official calls you to say that *your* child is having some trouble, you ought to believe him or her and address the problem. Many parents bristle because they think the school is suggesting that their child take medication, or that there is "something wrong" with their child, when, in fact, the prevailing message is that their child needs a little extra help and care.

Again, some of these things can be addressed by having your child sit in the front row of the class, or by requesting that a teacher not turn his or her back on the class when talking to the students. Simple adjustments by the teacher may help an ADD-type student pay attention in a classroom setting. However, you can do your part to help your child's education by realizing that the brain at school (and elsewhere) doesn't function as well when it's not fed well.

To make things easier for these stressed families, I developed a simple diet that focuses on redirecting families to healthier food options, because parents were overwhelmingly asking for very specific recommendations.

One of the hallmarks of ADD/ADHD is poor behavior at birthday parties. The combination of sweets and the need to cooperate in a large group of active children makes birthday parties nearly impossible for children with ADD/ADHD to handle. I've talked to so many parents who are very upset and saddened that their children just can't have fun at these social events. Parents often feel that their struggles are unique. Paradoxically, they are comforted to find out just how many families have this identical experience and problem. If all these parents were put in the same room, they'd be surprised to find that they echo one another when they begin speaking about their children. "He stopped getting invited to birthday parties. He was impossible." "He couldn't take turns." "He couldn't focus on pin the tail on the donkey; he'd go off somewhere else." They would all describe the same episodes: their child got to the party, went straight for the cupcakes and the candy, and threw a tantrum or two; soon the other kids wouldn't play with him or her. The parents decided to leave the party early.

The catalyst for all this is clearly the sugar. *Somehow, some way, please keep your child away from sugar.* On the way to the birthday party, have pretzels and apples and pears and almonds and walnuts. Feed your child proteins and complex carbohydrates, which slow food's absorption and digestion, and stop some of the roller-coaster high and low blood-sugar levels that children get from birthday-party food. Feed your child healthy food before the birthday party so that the edge is taken off his or her appetite. In fact, why not feed your child good, nutritious foods everywhere, every day? Why start with Ritalin and similar drugs? Older kids who exhibit the same symptoms that they showed when they were younger deserve developmental evaluations. Even then, why not start by changing your child's diet for ten days or even thirty days to start? There are no harmful physical side effects in enforcing a healthier sleep schedule for ten days. Please get your child out of the house every day for a week, away from the TV and into a park where he or she can run and play for an hour or more. Look into soccer teams or basketball leagues and gymnastics or dance classes. The whole family wins when everybody exercises more and when you show your child that there are going to be limits set and adhered to from now on.

The heart of the whole thing is really nutrition—the diet. Think of meals and snacks as the most natural medicine. Great nutrition makes the body run better, makes the mind think more clearly, and allows children to have more fun.

You Are What You Eat

When I was a child, I drank Coca-Cola in six-ounce bottles. That was bad enough. But today, children have no trouble finding twelve-, sixteen-, and thirty-two-ounce soft drinks loaded with sugar and caffeine. Supermarkets sometimes don't seem to have anything but sugar-loaded cereals that are colored and preserved with chemicals known to adversely affect brain function. Manufacturers realize that the best way to get a customer for life—or at least for childhood—is to put as much sugar in their products as possible. As parents, we are so thrilled to see our kids eat that we're oblivious to the deceptive labels and packaging that hide the truth about what we're putting in our kids' bodies. The sugar-filled cereals our children spoon voraciously into their mouths in the morning promise to provide a "day's worth of vitamins," but this nearly worthless amount of vitamins comes in chocolate-filled cocoa morsels. And yes, it's gotten worse. When I was a child, we sure couldn't find anything that remotely resembled the Oreo cereal kids throw into the shopping cart today. Nine out of ten cereals on the shelf—maybe even nineteen out of twenty—are sugar-based. Even worse, these sugary cereals are placed on the bottom shelves, at eye level for toddlers and children. While you're looking at the oatmeal on the top shelves in the breakfast-food aisle, your child is looking at the crapola chocolate-crunch cereals on the bottom shelves. The consumer watchdogs are very clear when they talk about Honey Bunches of Oats; there's not much honey in there—it's sugar.

Another important topic is relaxation. Children need to learn how to put themselves at ease during times of stress. They don't get enough time to relax. They are constantly under enormous stress to perform well. It's developmentally incorrect to pressure preschoolers and kindergartners to *master* basic reading at ages four, five, and six. This pressured learning environment highlights too many kids' learning differences and makes them feel bad about themselves.

Allow your child to develop naturally. Given a little more time to grow and develop, many kids who have been branded with ADD/ADHD might have adjusted to academics better, but our society likes to make one size fit all, and parents see natural learning differences at a young age as a sign of something worse. They pressure their children to do better and unwittingly create an intense environment that makes their children nervous and anxious. It doesn't let up as our children get older: there's middle school, then high school, then college, and then the workplace. There are social, emotional, and work-related pressures. Since we can't change this about our society, what we must do is make sure our children are prepared to perform comfortably within it, and the best way to do this is naturally—natural learning, natural whole foods, natural athleticism, and natural sleep patterns. Let's allow children to develop at a different pace than we're dictating now. Instead of asking all children to be able to read at the same time, let's embrace and appreciate all their differences instead of labeling them when they're *five years old.*

Very simply, there just aren't that many kids who need to be medicated.

Difficulties in school early on may simply call for transferring your child to a new school that has different teaching methods. There's no point in putting your children in a learning environment that makes them feel incompetent or unintelligent. This only leads to more frustration and pressure on the children, the educators, and the parents.

Children are more capable of understanding situations and their own conditions than we give them credit for. I don't have any trouble analogizing with an eight-year-old kid. When I ask him what his favorite car is, whether he says some fancy sports car or even a pickup truck, I say, "Would you put cheap fuel in that car? Are you going to fill it with cheap gas and cheap oil?" He laughs and says, "No, only the best."

I say, "Well, a pickup truck can't play soccer, can't shoot a jump shot, can't go to school, and can't dance ballet. Your body's better and more important than the pickup truck or the Porsche. Shouldn't you put the best food into your body?" The kids get it, even when the adults don't.

If this concept of good food and good health is comprehensible to children, should we adults have so much trouble with it? When we give our kids "fuel" that is composed of sugar and artificial sweeteners, colors, and preservatives, their days won't be as much fun, and their bodies can't possibly work as well.

We all know the brain is a very sophisticated organ. If it is subjected to a bad diet, it just doesn't work as well. The standard American child's diet shortens attention spans and decreases ability to learn and have fun in school. This sugar-filled, unnatural diet makes it difficult for children to make friends and play with those friends and to stay awake and alert in class. For a lot of children, poor nutrition has a huge negative impact; they're not as quick and they don't do as well at school as children who have healthier diets. The kids who are always teetering on the edge of misbehavior because they have attention deficit problems can completely lose the ability to compensate for the sudden fluctuations in their blood sugar and brain chemistry brought on by bad diet. If your child is being fed improperly at every meal, he or she is being kept in a constant and uncomfortable state of imbalance, and it's no wonder that he or she is always getting into trouble, getting stomachaches and headaches, and causing problems for others.

I have seen countless kids who did better in school, at home, on vacation, at parties, and in sports, once they were fed differently. And I still believe the simplest measures can yield the most dramatic gains.

Here's the Plan

Don't give your child sugar.

Eliminate sugar for one week if longer periods of time sound too daunting. We owe it to our kids to feed them the best food we can. If we are sincere about following this plan, our kids will respond positively. The change from a sugar-laden diet to a healthier one might not be easy, but if the entire family embraces better eating habits, the children will adapt.

In my office, I put a lot of time and energy into explaining the new diet to children. I relate it to performance in sports. I put it in terms of running faster, jumping higher, and having more fun in general. After the initial discussion and introduction, I explain the new diet in a very positive way. "Won't it be great to go to the market with Mom and Dad and pick out the freshest melons and the reddest strawberries? Won't your pancakes taste great topped with a big mountain of berries?"

Kids get it easily. If only the adults did.

I've seen preschool classes of fifteen children where there were some-how a hundred birthday-party days. I don't know how this happens . . . maybe my math is bad. Do I object to all the "special occasions" that seem to mandate sugar? No. I tell kids that, of course, we're not going to put birthday candles in a carrot. We're not going to have a birthday carrot. We're not going to sing "Happy carrot to you!" It's a birthday party, and there's going to be a birthday cake. But there doesn't need to be cake followed by a quart of soda, followed by ice cream, cookies, cupcakes, and candy. There are birthday parties and parties for Easter, Hanukkah, and Valentine's Day. There are dozens of days when it's expected that kids will eat things that are packed with sugar. In my office checkups, however, I like to remind kids that while sometimes there will be sugar, most of the time there are strawberries, grapes, apples, pears, and peaches to choose from. They listen. They get it.

I like children to have choices, but there are certain situations in which their judgment cannot prevail. We never ask a three- or a four-year-old if he or she thinks that holding hands while crossing a street is a good idea. We simply hold the child's hand. Likewise, I don't think a three- or a four-year-old should decide whether he or she should eat sugar-frosted cocoa junk for breakfast every day. One is obviously an issue of short-term health and safety and the other is an issue of longer-term health and safety.

In the case of extreme food intolerances, what children eat could truly harm them. If a child has diabetes, he or she *can't* eat certain foods at a birthday party. You're not depriving that child, and it's not excessive for a parent to say, "Johnny has diabetes, so he's going to skip the cake."

But what if Johnny has ADD/ADHD or something that looks like it? Then it's likely that everyone's reaction is less empathetic. You'll proba-bly hear something along the lines of "Aw, come on. Just let the kid have some cake." What most people don't understand is that the cake and the other sugar-filled foods take the fun out of the birthday party for Johnny. That the cake, the candy, and the ice cream are not rewards. They amount to a punishment. We parents know that this much sugar guaran-tees disruptive behavior, tears, tantrums, and lost friendships.

And maybe no invitation to the next birthday party.

You're not being a "bad" parent by trying to substitute watermelon and fruit salad for the cake. By allowing his body to be safe and healthier, you are doing the most you can to increase his enjoyment of the party, and furthermore, you're teaching him how to manage his health.

And that's what we're trying to accomplish.

2

What Is ADD/ADHD and Does Your Child Really Have It?

Parents are rarely taken by surprise when they receive a call from a teacher at their child's preschool, kindergarten, or elementary school telling them that their son or daughter is having trouble behaving or handling academic demands. When their child has trouble at school, parents have usually seen the signs of inattention, hyperactivity, and especially impulse control in their toddler long before the child's first day at school or in a new class. In the middle of playing with another child, their son or daughter may suddenly wander off, drop a toy or a game for no reason, have trouble sharing balls or books with another child, or lose control completely and ignore all efforts to get him or her to calm down.

Sometimes, parents even suspect—before the school calls—that their child's symptoms may point to ADD/ADHD or a similar problem. But as long as their child is at home, or with family and friends, places where there are often as many adults around as children, situations like these are easier to control or avoid. Besides, children mature at different rates, and their personalities, temperaments, and energy levels vary considerably, so it can be hard for parents to distinguish an outbreak of the so-called terrible twos from a sign of a more serious underlying problem. Moreover, even if they suspect a behavioral disorder, parents often hope their child will "outgrow" it before preschool or kindergarten. I have watched families resist change and remain in denial for a long time. I try very hard to shorten this period of denial.

One family I had the pleasure of helping comes to mind. Their youngest son, Andrew, was lovable and full of energy from the moment he could walk. At home, his hyperactive excitability provided hours of entertainment for his parents and siblings. He was always full of giggly laughter and would dash around the house and make lots of loud noise. This childish behavior that the family always found endearing (if sometimes irritating), however, persisted past the age when other kids had seemed to gain more control of themselves. Because he was so young,

What Does ADD/ADHD Mean?

Attention deficit disorder/attention deficit hyperactivity disorder (ADD/ADHD) is a condition affecting children and adults that is characterized by problems with attention, impulsivity, and sometimes overactivity. The "H" in ADHD stands for hyperactivity, and sometimes parents are confused by this diagnosis because they think that "hyperactivity" and the condition of ADD in general are synonymous. Because we now know the condition often manifests as a combination of inattention and impulsivity without any overt hyperactivity, the two separate designations are needed. ADHD is used to specify the condition when it is accompanied by hyperactivity, and technically speaking, ADD implies the condition in the absence of hyperactivity. Colloquially, however, the two variations are often referred to together under the general umbrella of "ADD."

ADD and ADHD affect from 3 to 7 percent of school-age children and anywhere from 2 to 4 percent of adults. Some reports, however, reflect that this percentage may be even higher.

ADD and ADHD are the current diagnostic labels for a condition that has been recognized and studied for over a century. Over the years, it has been known by several other names, including brain damaged syndrome, minimal brain dysfunction, and hyperkinetic impulsive disorder. Science recognizes three subtypes of ADHD: inattentive, hyperactive-impulsive, and combined. A diagnosis of one type or another depends on the specific symptoms—that is, the "diagnostic criteria"—that person has.

Whereas an accurate diagnosis of ADD/ADHD can be the first step toward treating the condition, misdiagnosis and inappropriate treatment—*which occur more than half the time*—can be a destructive and often devastating process for a family. This doesn't need to happen, but with many pediatricians and parents looking for quick fixes to an overwhelming problem, too often it does.

his parents dismissed his behavior as a phase he would outgrow or as a natural feature of his personality.

You're probably thinking that playfulness and rowdiness are typical of most young children—and you're right. Parents take for granted that this is normal, and in most cases it is. Signs that the child's behavior should be watched with more caution usually emerge once he or she enters school.

When children begin preschool, the new demands made on them when they're surrounded by new faces in unfamiliar surroundings may overwhelm kids with poor impulse control. The school isn't concerned about academic performance in four- and five-year-olds. Despite the increase in emphasis on learning over play in preschool and kindergarten, it is rare that a child "fails" for academic reasons at this stage. The problems usually surface over behavioral issues: the child just isn't getting along with the other children, doesn't pay attention to teachers' instructions, can't complete simple tasks, or is getting into fights.

Andrew's parents sought help for him when the behavior that they found so lovable at home turned out to be disruptive and clearly abnormal when he was among his preschool peers. Although he was timid and reserved at first, within a month of being in the classroom setting, Andrew would duck underneath the table during class, stand on top of his chair when the teacher was talking—he just wouldn't sit still. He couldn't quite grasp the concept of raising his hand before answering questions, no matter how many times the teacher reminded him.

His teacher recognized the signs of what she thought was ADD/ADHD, so she felt the need to inform Andrew's parents of the possibility. They were able to get an official diagnosis soon after and sought expert help at a time when Andrew's behaviors were easiest to modify and his condition easiest to treat. With proper dietary changes and the encouragement of proper, healthy behavior at home, I am happy to report that Andrew was able to control the most disruptive of his symptoms by the time he entered the first grade.

Whether parents notice the warning signs themselves or are alerted to them by their child's teacher, the school psychologist, or an administrator, their first step should be to get another expert's opinion about whether their child needs further evaluation. Young children spend a lot of time with teachers, and teachers have the training and experience that allow them to differentiate among children behaving appropriately and inappropriately for their ages.

Your child's school shouldn't dictate your family's decisions about health care—you're in charge in that area. However, teachers can serve as an invaluable early warning system for problems with your son or daughter's behavior, and you should consult with them when making your decision about what is best for your child.

The teacher's call, then, should obviously be taken seriously. Frequently, you already know about the problem, and now that someone else has confirmed it, you need to deal with it. Many parents contact my office because they've received a call about possible ADD/ADHD in their child and they just don't know what to do. Your pediatrician is one of the professionals you can consult to assess whether your child has attention deficit/hyperactivity disorder or is just immature or perhaps in the wrong school. Child psychologists and psychiatrists can also play a role in making a diagnosis.

Most children with ADD/ADHD create disturbances in the classroom. They act out, physically or verbally; are uncooperative; or impulsively strike or kick a classmate. At the beginning of the school year, especially for students starting school for the first time, the new faces and new environment are enough to keep their attention. For a month or

What Causes ADD/ADHD?

There are few definitive answers as to what causes ADD/ADHD. However, research has demonstrated that ADD/ADHD has a very strong neurobiological basis. Heredity may make the largest contribution to a child's tendency to ADD/ADHD.

In instances where heredity does not seem to be a factor, difficulties during pregnancy, prenatal exposure to alcohol and tobacco, premature delivery, significantly low birth weight, excessively high lead levels, and postnatal injury to the brain have all been found to be risk factors for ADD/ADHD.

Many health-care professionals believe that ADD/ADHD (or behavior that mimics it) arises from excessive sugar intake, food additives, excessive television viewing, inadequate limit setting, or social and environmental factors such as poverty or family chaos.

even six weeks, the child is engaged and cooperative. Then the novelty wears off, and the demands of interacting with classmates intensify or exhaustion settles in. These are usually the conditions that cause a child to hit or kick another child without warning or provocation.

Similar things can also happen with children who don't really have ADD/ADHD. A child who is having attention or control issues because his or her breakfast cereal causes wide blood-sugar fluctuations can be the reason that child loses self-control and hits another student, grabs a toy from his or her neighbor, or creates a disturbance. Some students are never aggressive, but they suffer from the *inattentive* form of ADD/ADHD. These children may escape notice for years, especially in classrooms where the teachers have their hands full with more hyper kids.

Getting a Proper Diagnosis

ADD/ADHD is a serious health issue. The first thing on your list should be to get an accurate diagnosis as soon as possible in order to start addressing the problem and to avoid treatment that is not appropriate, doesn't help, or might even be harmful.

When I talk to parents about ADD/ADHD, I have to be careful not to be too lighthearted about the diagnosis, because I myself have a very serious unmedicated case of ADD. Because I have a very organized wife, an excellent office manager, and, of course, a great diet, my life works quite well in spite of the condition. (I *am* late a lot, though.)

A correct diagnosis resolves confusion about the causes of the child's problems. It lets parents and the child move forward with their lives with more accurate information about what is wrong and what can be done to help. Once ADD/ADHD or ADD/ADHD-like behavior is diagnosed, the child and his or her family can begin treatment for their body, their mind, and their environment. Parents may be able to work with school staff to reduce stress in the classroom, find a more appropriate classroom setting, select the right treatment(s), and make adjustments in family life that help them better manage their child's behavior and enjoy him or her more.

The First Three Questions to Ask

There are lots of questions parents can ask and a number of behavioral signs to look for when they think their child may have ADD/ADHD. In my office, however, I always ask the following three questions:

1. What does the school say about your child?

2. How does your child do at birthday parties?

3. Who is your child's best friend?

School—whether preschool or kindergarten—is the first social setting a child encounters away from the protective umbrella of parents and other familiar caregivers, siblings, and close relatives. It is the first environment in which a child gets socialized to the "real world." A teacher's authority must be accepted in order for the school system to work. Your child must learn to cooperate with his or her classmates.

Now, not all of us gets along with everyone all the time. In fact, no one does. We can all think of bosses we've disliked, coworkers who have rubbed us the wrong way, and people we just could never, in a million years, get along with. However, schools are training grounds for life, and school administrators monitor interactions among students carefully. When parents tell me that their child's teacher has phoned to alert them to their child's disruptive behavior in the classroom, I know what might be coming. The next step will be another phone call, a meeting, a strong request for an evaluation, and, eventually, medication.

In the earlier part of my career, I thought I was leaping to the child's defense by telling the parents that the teacher wasn't right for the child, that the school wasn't right for the child, and that all children have bad days. I've stopped doing that. Even though any of those three things might be true, I've learned to listen very closely to what a teacher says about a child.

The answer to the second question, "How does your child do at birthday parties?" may hold the key to explaining the child's "bad" behavior. Birthday parties present children with stumbling blocks: lack of structure, junk food, sugar, and the need to follow directions and cooperate with peers. For a child with ADD/ADHD or similar symptoms, these are ingredients for disaster. Children with ADD/ADHD often fall apart in social settings like birthday parties. Their symptoms get worse, the other children tease and exclude them, and pretty soon they find themselves left off invitation lists for future parties.

When I ask these children who their best friends are, they sometimes reply with a name the parents haven't heard before. "Johnny," a child might say, and the amazed parent exclaims, "Who's Johnny?" If the scene plays out this way, I know that the child's behavioral problems are damaging his or her social life. The question is valuable to me as I evaluate kids because even though they know they're expected to have friends, and they're aware that their peers and siblings have them, these kids have lots of trouble making friends. And because they don't want to admit this (and who would?), they panic and will blurt out a random name. Children can be brutal when it comes to excluding the quirkier of their classmates. It happens, it stings, and it keeps stinging. As parents, it's heartbreaking when we discover that it's happening to our kids, but when we do find out, we know it's time to make a change.

What Should Parents and/or Caregivers Look For?

Inattention, hyperactivity, and impulsivity are early red flags. At two years of age, this is completely normal behavior. But by age three, these things should be tapering off. Long before a child starts school, some parents notice that the child loses interest in the middle of playing a game or watching TV, runs around completely out of control, or acts without thinking, often at personal risk or risk to other children around him or her. Children mature at different rates and vary widely in personality, temperament, and energy levels, so these signs are clues that something might be wrong, but they are *not* conclusive proof of ADD/ADHD. When home, school, and social problems arise, we may need an expert's opinion about whether the behavior is appropriate for the child's age. We need to examine the child's diet. And we need to look at how the parents set boundaries. Parents can ask their child's pediatrician or a child psychologist or psychiatrist to assess whether this is attention deficit/hyperactivity disorder or, more likely at young ages, is just natural behavior.

When the Signs Point to Behavioral Problems

If ADD/ADHD is suspected, start by talking with your child's pediatrician. The next step is a more detailed evaluation to determine whether the child has ADD, ADHD, or another condition. Some pediatricians do the assessment themselves, but most refer their patients to a mental-health specialists such as a pediatric developmentalist, a psychologist, a psychiatrist, or even a neurologist.

In most states, the school system has an obligation to assess your child at no cost to you. But you might also choose private evaluation if you feel this suits you and your family better.

Diagnosing ADD/ADHD at Different Grade Levels

Parents, teachers, and health-care professionals can observe a child's behavior, evaluate that behavior, and then decide if that behavior is appropriate or inappropriate for a given age group. Preschool and kindergarten are great times to make certain that your child is not "falling behind" or having social trouble because of behavior. Nobody wants labels applied at that early age, or maybe at any age. But it helps a child to have adults actively interested and involved in modifying behavior that is causing problems.

Many children make it through preschool and kindergarten unscathed, thanks to teachers who are dedicated and talented and love what they do. No one goes into teaching kindergarten for the money. These teachers have a gift for handling the often unpredictable behavior of five-year-olds, the academic bar is still set pretty low, and the environment continues to be fairly informal. Signs of behavioral problems, ADD and similar conditions, can show up even at this age, but it's in first or second grade when children are overwhelmed by the organizational demands of having to study several subjects, the expectation that they'll begin to master reading and writing, and the need to keep track of assignments and to do homework. When their health is not at its optimum because of a steady diet of junk food or lack of exercise, their weakened impulse control also can't handle the demands of interactions in the lunchroom, on the playing field, and outside school.

Some children with ADD/ADHD or similar attention deficits manage to scrape through the first three elementary school grades, but they run into trouble in the fourth grade. Most schools increase academic demands and give kids more responsibility for keeping track of schoolwork. Social and athletic demands increase, too. Some kids fall apart at this stage, with full-blown symptoms of ADD/ADHD erupting, as if overnight.

If I were your child's pediatrician and I resisted the diagnosis of ADD/ADHD up to this point, I was probably wrong. If parents resisted the diagnosis, they have to change. We have to do it together.

A very nice family who had recently immigrated to the United States came to me with their eleven-year-old daughter, Liza. She was a real handful in the classroom—talking loudly in class, being short-tempered and an extremely poor sport on the playground, and having emotional outbursts whenever she felt challenged by difficult assignments. She was often insulting to her classmates. Liza's parents were notified by school administrators that their daughter's behavior had become unmanageable. Their solution was to enroll her in a different private school. They hoped that the clean slate would be just what their daughter needed to get her footing and start anew. After a miserable social experience and academic failure at this school, her parents had run out of options. Afraid of what their friends would think if their child was officially branded with a "mental disorder," they put off getting a diagnosis until it became clear that Liza was not going to outgrow what they finally accepted was ADD/ADHD.

Delaying treatment had hurt Liza emotionally and created self-esteem problems. She felt increasingly inadequate and had been caught trying to cheat on tests or copying off other students' assignments. She simply felt that she was "too dumb" to do assignments on her own. Years of being teased and left out by her peers had made her insecure and angry. Moving from one school to another had taken away a sense of stability and made it harder than ever to make friends. Furthermore, as she was old enough to recognize social norms and understand the ways she had difficulty conforming to them, she had begun to accept that she was just "weird" and that there was something wrong with her.

Liza was a difficult child to treat because no one had gotten to the root of her problems, allowing them to grow for years. Her condition called for more than medication, diet, and family changes. She needed therapy. And her success in overcoming ADD/ADHD depended on her receiving help with her self-esteem issues and recognizing that while she had learning differences she wasn't stupid. With the help of great nutrition, a good family therapist, and her parents' increased understanding of ADD/ADHD, she was able to enroll in a high school where she has a normal social life and gets decent grades. If we had addressed her problems earlier, it might have been easier to treat them.

When I began writing this book, I wanted to make all the chapters really short. Why? Because parents of children with ADD often have ADD! This presents another layer to this complex problem, because an adult with ADD/ADHD may unwittingly be modeling undesirable behavior for his or her children. In these cases, I work with the entire family to address all of these health concerns.

Understanding Medical Treatment

For years we wondered why *stimulant* medication made hyperactive kids less "hyper." There are also nonstimulant drugs for ADHD/ADD, which I prescribe much less frequently because of their inefficacy and side effects. Now we know that stimulant medications mainly stimulate the executive center of the frontal lobe. This is the part of the brain that is in charge of impulse control. Making the frontal lobe more active helps quiet ADD/ADHD behavior.

If your child's ADD/ADHD or other emotional problem is severe and poses a physical danger to him or her and to other children, prompt and proper administration of drug treatment is, of course, recommended, but it is always with the hope of eventually taking your child off of these medications.

3

The ADD/ADHD Cure
Handbook

You know your child needs extra care, and you have a good idea of what you need to do to provide that extra care, but you're not exactly sure how to go about doing it. If *The ADD and ADHD Cure* tells you *why*, this chapter—the handbook portion of the book—tells you exactly *how*. Here, you will find a full explanation of the ADD/ADHD cure, shopping and food preparation tips, a thirty-day meal plan designed to take all the guesswork out of what to serve at mealtimes, and, best of all, more than a hundred wonderful and simple recipes for you to enjoy. Let's get started.

It All Starts with Diet: The Cure Explained

You may have already begun medication to treat your child's ADD/ADHD. Although this isn't my first choice, I'm not suggesting that you did anything wrong or that you did a disservice to your child. The school may have pressured you to make a decision, or perhaps you felt hurried to change things as soon as possible. Maybe you were led to believe that medication was the only answer for treating ADD/AHD.

Whether your child has been on medication for a long time, is just beginning to take it, or if you're still considering your options, we can all agree that a thirty-day commitment to an alternative treatment or even just a ten-day trial is not drastic or radical. It may eliminate the need for medication, or at the very least allow a reduced dose and therefore reduced side effects. A lifetime of popping pills, however, is drastic.

I've built my pediatric practice around my belief that while drugs can be one of the temporary treatments for ADD/ADHD and similar behavioral disorders, proper diet and a healthy lifestyle might provide the cure for ADHD. I've seen countless children successfully shed the ADHD label and turn their lives around. Feeding your child a proper diet and encouraging exercise might seem difficult at first, but it's our job as parents to help our children make positive changes even when they're reluctant.

Eating a healthy diet creates lifelong benefits well beyond decreasing or eliminating school and social problems. I cringe at the word "diet" because it implies inflexible eating limits and deprivation from familiar foods that we've learned to enjoy without worry. "Diet" is used differently in this book and in medicine in general. It implies a pattern of eating and fulfilling certain nutritional and behavioral goals. There are four important guidelines.

1. No processed sugar.

2. No artificial flavorings and colorants.

3. No foods that are dairy-based.

4. No foods containing gluten.

With a little bit of vigilance, you will get tremendous results, I promise. I've seen them.

I realize that the change will be greater for some families than for others. If your child eats fruit-flavored sugar cereal and doughnuts for breakfast, the shift to a sugar-free diet will be more challenging, because the switch will amount to a lifestyle change, but the benefits will be hugely noticeable. For families already feeding their children a pretty healthy diet, making some modifications shouldn't prove too hard. For those parents who have been prevented from feeding their children the healthiest of foods for one reason or another, keep in mind that there is *nothing* radical about good nutrition, but there are few things as risky as blindly taking medication.

You'll see encouraging improvements within seven to ten days, but please stay committed for thirty days to see really great results.

It bears repeating: *the first step in the diet is to eliminate all processed sugar.* Feel free to eat lots of fruit, but get rid of cookies, cakes, candy, sugary cereals, and artificially flavored drinks. Processed sugar has no nutritive value. It's been milled and distilled over and over until it is an empty shell of addictive, unhealthy flavor. Why are the natural sugars found in fruit okay? Because this wonderful sweetness is absorbed in a matrix—a framework, that is—of fiber and water. Fruit is 90 percent water by weight. This and the fiber allow for slow, gradual absorption and none of the wild blood-sugar bounces that are causing your child to misbehave all this time.

In contrast to any acceptable amount of natural sugar, large doses of processed sugar—such as the amounts added to kids' cereals, packaged treats, sodas, and juices—produce a rapid change. Insulin levels spike and then inevitably crash. Moods become harder to control. Depression sets in. Exhaustion sets in. Emotions can fluctuate, and this can happen to *anyone* who punishes his or her body with large doses of processed sugars. In people with ADD/ADHD, these problems are greatly magnified.

So . . . no cookies, cakes, candies, or ice cream! I mean it.

Instead, your child can become accustomed to getting his or her sweets and treats from fruit. This simple adjustment saves your child from the artificial bounce—and then crash—that he or she suffers from when getting heavy, regular doses of refined sugar.

Sugary treats are everywhere. Kids today bring to school lunch boxes full of foods that have more sugar content than nutritional value. Teachers hand sugary foods out as rewards to students—a practice I find ridiculous. Halloween and other holidays are devoted to celebrating with sugar, not just for the day but for weeks, until the sugar stash is depleted. It's challenging to wean your child off sugar. The school, the parties, and even the calendar seem to be conspiring against you.

Changing your child's diet is challenging but far from impossible, and as long as you are honest with your child about why he or she needs to refuse candy from friends and even teachers, you'll succeed together. Be honest with friends and teachers as well about why they need to stop offering these behavior-changing foods to your child. Explain to others why there is a crisp red apple packed in your child's lunch box while his or her classmates have pudding cups and cans of soda. In my practice, I have the most success when I am honest, positive, and playful with children. I tell them, "Your body is like an expensive car that can go faster than any animal on the planet. It is shiny and new. It lets you do all the things you love doing and will keep getting stronger and better and faster. You could be the best soccer player you ever wanted to be. You could be a prima ballerina. Let's only put the *best* fuel in this car—your body, your muscles, your bones, your brain—okay?"

Kids understand this right off, but adults seem to get it a little more slowly. Kids really do buy into the idea of getting stronger and healthier because of good food. My discussions with three-year-olds, six-year-olds, and ten-year-olds are honest. Maybe the discussions are filled with exaggerations, but they are also filled with plenty of truth. Remember, children are more likely to stick with the program if we include them in the decision to follow it.

The next step is taking your family off dairy products and wheat for thirty days. It is estimated that 30 to 35 percent of people have sensitivities to gluten (the major protein in wheat and certain other grains), and an astounding 50 to 80 percent of people have sensitivities to dairy. Doctors have known for decades that kids with dairy and gluten sensitivities behave differently when exposed to these foods, and there are far more children with these sensitivities than we are aware of. Although the statistics for dairy sensitivity are constantly debated, it has been medically proven that by age six or seven, the level of the enzyme lactase that processes dairy drops, which makes dairy digestion difficult for some people and even impossible for others. In fact, our bodies can treat the milk like an invader, and our immune system attempts to fight it by producing antibodies. Medical research has shown that in susceptible children, early exposure to cow's milk increases the instance of diabetes.

Surprising? It shouldn't be. In addition to the above, unless you buy organic milk, the milk you're drinking is tainted with recombinant bovine growth hormone (rBGH), antibiotics, and other chemicals. Most countries (Canada, Japan, New Zealand, Australia, and all twenty-five nations of the European Union) have banned rBGH because of its known detrimental effect on health. Even if you are buying organic milk and only eating organic dairy products, there is this to consider: milk comes from cows and was created by Mother Nature for baby cows. By drinking their mothers' milk and processing it with their *four* stomachs, calves double their body weight in only forty-seven days and usually live very short lives. It's no wonder that *our* bodies treat milk like an alien substance.

In most people, dairy intolerance and gluten sensitivity cause mild discomfort. The effects on kids with ADD/ADHD are worse and simply not worth it. Their bodies may react to these allergens and stop the absorption of nutrients. These foods can also cause intestinal inflammation and alter mood and behavior.

Banning dairy can be difficult—in some cases, even more difficult than banning sugar—but it's worth it. Most of us have been raised to believe that consuming a tall glass of milk is healthy and nutritious. It's not. Most of us have been raised to believe that eating whole-wheat bread is healthy and nutritious. For many children, it's the opposite.

Finally, discontinuing the use of artificial sweeteners, flavorings, and colors has been proven to change behavior, as reported in reputable medical journals. These chemicals resemble neurotransmitters in the brain, and their adverse effect on body and brain function has been discussed in the medical community for decades. Recent studies conducted by British researchers at the University of Southampton have linked artificial food additives specifically to hyperactivity in children. In the study, three hundred participants were fed juices spiked with artificial sweeteners and preservatives, and then they were observed. Researchers concluded in the study (published in the *Lancet* medical journal in 2007) that "adverse effects are not just seen in children with extreme hyperactivity (such as ADHD) but can also be seen in the general population and across the range of severities of hyperactivity."

My experience and the experience of the families in my practice have left no doubt in my mind: artificially flavored and colored foods should be removed from our children's diets because of what these ingredients do to their brains.

These are big steps for a family that eats a lot of processed or packaged foods. Your kids will do great on this diet, and you will, too. Tell the kids what they *can* eat, not what they *can't* eat. View this as an adventure in a new way of eating, rather than something meant to limit or punish. Even if "adventure" isn't a word your children would use, they can still embrace healthy eating habits. The second part of this chapter will show you how to make healthy, tasty, easy-to-prepare meals. We give you shopping tips and more than a hundred recipes, as well as a day-by-day meal plan.

This thirty-day "vacation" from sugar, dairy, wheat, and artificial additives will make your whole family feel better, from the youngest

Get Your Child Involved

Children are more excited about their diet if they feel that they are actively participating in creating it. Here are some ideas:

- Let your child look through recipe books and online with you; together, you can choose new foods to try.

- Set up a pizza (with soy cheese or no cheese) or pasta bar where the kids can choose what ingredients they want. They are much more likely to eat foods that "they" made. The more hands-on a meal is, the more fun for the child.

- Let your child put together his or her own snacks.

Make Sprouts

Children will be more excited to eat foods that they grow themselves. One simple activity is making sprouts. Start by putting a half cup of lentils (or mung beans, alfalfa seeds, or sunflower seeds) in a jar with a wide neck, then covering with purified water. Cut a piece of cheesecloth to fit generously over the jar's neck and secure it with a rubber band. Soak the beans or seeds for one hour, then pour out the water through the cheesecloth. Shake the jar gently to distribute the seeds as evenly as possible, and let the jar sit on its side in a shady place. Wet the seeds and pour out the water (remove the cheesecloth first, but put it back) three or four times a day. You don't have to soak them again. Some beans sprout within forty-eight hours; some take a few more days. When the sprouts have little green tips, eat them! Put uneaten sprouts in a container in the refrigerator. They will last for five days.

member to the oldest. You'll find that your child will have an increase in the healthiest kind of energy and an increased ability to focus at school and at home.

We have no excuses. Let's do it.

The ADD/ADHD Cure Diet Guide

I am fortunate that my wife, Meyera, does all the meal planning and cooking. Because we both lead busy lives, she has come up with quick, uncomplicated, and very tasty meals for us. Meyera understands the importance of healthy, well-balanced choices, and on the following pages, she is going to share them with you.

The best way to make this plan work is to get the whole family on board. That is why there is a large number of recipes from which to select. Choose what suits your tastes, time schedule, and age group. We remember well all the different, repetitive meals as our child's tastes changed. You will find a variety of options to which you can add and subtract ingredients and quantities and even serve at different meal-times. Who's to say that hot cereal can't be dinner and leftover burritos can't be breakfast?

I've divided the next section into three parts.

The first section offers a selection of preparation tips to help you start the ADD/ADHD cure off right for the whole family. This section contains essential information on what ingredients to avoid, tips on how to prepare foods naturally (and how to prepare natural foods!), and guidelines on how to read labels so that you can shop smart and shop healthy. There are a few charts for your reference. Most packages of beans and rice provide serving amounts and cooking times. If you buy in bulk, this information will help. Incidentally, buying in bulk is less expensive and you'll always have extra on hand.

The second section is a thirty-day meal plan. It includes suggested dishes for every meal of the day from breakfast to dinner, plus snacks and even dessert. Even though the plan lays out everything neatly, to take all the guesswork out of mealtime, feel free to mix and match what works for you. The goal of this section is to make life's food choices easier as you travel through this transition toward a healthier way of eating.

The third section contains recipes. The majority of the recipes are vegetarian with some fish, chicken, and meat options. There is no wheat or dairy. (There are great-tasting soy options for smoothies and even whipped cream!)

My wife and I don't use a lot of fancy cooking equipment. She loves her wok, large frying pan (in which she never fries), large soup pot, good knife, paring knife, and good cooking spoons. She also uses a couple of baking trays and ice cube or frozen dessert trays.

So let's begin by taking a look at the items in your pantry and refrigerator. In order for this new program to work successfully, everything that has sugar, wheat, or dairy should be tossed out. Any foods containing artificial flavors or sweeteners also need to be discarded. Read all the ingredients on anything that is packaged or canned. This exercise could send you into shock, so be prepared. Many popular items are laden with high-fructose corn syrup and hidden wheat, not to mention artificial ingredients. Keep in mind that although you needn't go completely organic, it's a good idea to buy fresh fruits and vegetables whenever possible. Think "clean" and "pure."

If you want more flexibility with the meal plan, look over the menus and recipes and decide how to customize the meals to suit your family.

If you're customizing your meals, or foregoing the meal plan provided in this book in favor of preparing your own meals based on the guidelines, it helps to make your own shopping list. (One is provided for you here if you're following the meal plan.) If you have a co-op or an organic supermarket, I suggest starting there. Nowadays there is such a push for organic foods that many regular markets have organic sections and

Rethink the Way You Eat

Traditionally, Americans eat three meals a day and build their meals around a main dish. However, there is no need to feel constrained by this model. Why not build a meal out of side dishes, which are quicker to make? In addition, instead of serving three large meals a day, you can serve smaller meals and incorporate two or three snacks so that your child's energy remains at a more constant level throughout the day.

gluten-free foods. Most of the ingredients in my recipes are fresh, so even if, for instance, organic spinach is more expensive than the inorganic variety, you won't be buying potato chips or 24-ounce plastic containers of soda. You will find that once you get the hang of this plan, it can be smooth sailing.

If your supermarket does not carry organic products or have a gluten-free section, ask for it. You'd be surprised to learn that many people have your same concerns and have probably asked already. The more stores hear from you, the more they are inclined to satisfy you.

Conditioning Your Kids to Eat Healthy

Getting rid of milk, cheese, junk food, and sweets will make your child protest, but don't be discouraged. Young children *and* older children are still developing their tastes, and they can change. Teens and adults can more easily handle the rationale behind this book and recognize the great benefits. In tackling this challenge, here are a few things to remember:

- Kids can understand the importance of eating their vegetables if you explain it to them the right way. They respond with laughter during my office checkups when I say to them, "The first time *I* ate broccoli, do you think I liked it? The *next* time I ate broccoli, do you think I liked it? The *NEXT* time I ate broccoli, do you think I liked it? Why did I keep eating broccoli if I didn't like it? Because people whom I knew and trusted kept saying to me: 'Broccoli makes you faster, makes you stronger, makes you smarter. Broccoli tastes great. Try it again!' Guess what? Now I love broccoli and I eat it every day. And you know, it really does make you stronger and faster and smarter. Now then, the first time I ate spinach, do you think I liked it . . .?"

- Kids watch what their parents eat. Younger children watch what older children eat. Let your children see you enjoy (or pretend to enjoy) steamed vegetables, tofu, and hummus. Let them see you enjoy fresh raspberries, crunchy red apples, and a frozen strawberry dessert.

- Ease them into it: keep serving sizes small and the pressure low. Let's keep the explanations few in number, and the enthusiasm at a high level.

- Do not underestimate your child's palate and feel the need to dumb down foods to child level by serving only fish sticks and hot dogs. Although the recipes in this chapter may seem more grown-up, you'd be surprised by what children will enjoy, especially if they see you eating the same thing and if you're very clear about why you're doing it.

- Our children don't need to love all these changes, but if you're consistent, eventually they'll like them and the results.

Tips for Getting Your Kids to Eat Vegetables

My best tip for getting your kids to eat vegetables is to pretend you don't care whether they do or not. Eat vegetables in front of them, offer them vegetables, eat the ones that are left on their plate, and smile throughout.

But of course, if that doesn't work immediately, here are a few practical points and ideas:

- Cut up fruits and vegetables (or buy them precut) and keep them in the fridge in individual containers. Your kids are much more likely to snack on them if they're easily accessible.

- While you're cooking, put a salad or vegetables on the dining table. Kids will be much more willing to eat these foods to satisfy their hunger while they are waiting for dinner to be ready.

- When possible, buy local, seasonal, and organic produce.

- Puree vegetables and add them to pasta sauce or mashed potatoes so kids get the extra nutrition without knowing it.

- Make salsa with chunks of tomato, onion, green peppers, corn, and other vegetables to your liking. Dipping corn tortilla chips in salsa makes kids feel like they are having a treat.

- Try steaming artichokes, and then let your kids tear off the leaves and dip them in a sauce of some sort. An interactive vegetable makes eating healthfully more fun.

Easy Preparation Tips to Make Life Easier for You

The shopping and cooking in our plan may be different from what you're used to, but they can become easy and second nature very quickly. The transition is even faster if you use these preparation tips.

- Purees are all the rage now, and for good reason. They're handy, and they can be mixed together or into other dishes, served on top of or alongside other foods, or eaten straight up. Puree sweet potatoes, yams, and carrots together to mix into pasta sauce, stir into tomato soup, or spread on top of a multigrain bagel. Puree spinach and peas, or cauliflower and zucchini, together to mix into guacamole or to season with lemon juice and spices for a tasty veggie dip. Or puree beans for a fresh bean dip. Puree fruits and pack them into frozen dessert trays to make tasty frozen treats. Purees can typically be stored in the refrigerator for up to three days if you add a dash of lemon juice. Otherwise, they can be frozen and later thawed whenever you need them.

- Make extra. Instead of cooking every meal, make a few large meals a week and store them in the refrigerator so you don't have to cook every day. Consider this option especially when making soup or oatmeal.

- When cutting up vegetables for dinner, put a small portion of the raw chunks or pieces into a small container and refrigerate. If you use a blender or a food processor to make quick dip and store it alongside the veggies, you'll have a snack handy for when your kids get hungry in between meals.

- A lot of healthy recipes, including the ones found here, call for cooked grains, but if you've never cooked grains before, doing so can be something of a mystery. On the next page there is a handy guide to show you how to cook them al dente. Remember that grains don't need to be soaked before cooking.

- If you're cutting down the amount of meat you're feeding your child as part of the diet, beans will be a vital source of protein. And if you're just as confused about how to cook beans as you are about grains, there is a chart for that, too. Beans, unlike grains, need to be soaked overnight or at least six hours before cooking.

HOW TO COOK GRAINS

Grain (1 cup)	Water in Cups	Cooking Time	Yield in Cups
Barley	1-2½	40 minutes; let stand for 10 minutes covered	3
Basmati rice	1–2	20 minutes; let stand for 10 minutes	2½
Buckwheat oats	1–2	20–30 minutes	2
Bulgar	1-1½	20–30 minutes	2½
Couscous	1-1¾	15 minutes	1½
Millet	1–2	40 minutes	3¼
Quinoa	1–2	15 minutes; let stand for 10 minutes	3
Short-grain brown rice	1–2	40 minutes covered; let stand for 20 minutes covered	3
Tabouleh	1½–2, boiling	20 minutes; let stand for 10 minutes	2½
Triticale	1–3	1½ hours; let stand for 20 minutes	2½

HOW TO COOK BEANS

Beans (1 cup)	Water in Cups	Cooking Time	Yield in Cups
Adzuki	4½	1¾ hours	3
Black	3	1¼ hours	2½
Garbanzo	6½	3½ hours	3
Kidney	4	1½–2 hours	2½
Pinto	5	1½–2 hours	2½
Red	4	1½–2 hours	2½
Soy	6	3 hours	2½
White	5	2 hours	2½

Shopping for the Cure: Avoid the Traps

I always recommend preparing meals with fresh produce and natural ingredients as the best way to feed a child with ADD/ADHD. Unfortunately, some people have schedules so hectic they can't afford to cook meals from scratch every single time. Elements of your meal might have to include ready-made items from a supermarket shelf. When shopping, we always want to find the most natural, healthy options available.

Unfortunately, when you're standing in the food aisles, your better judgment is pitted against the misleading and persuasive food packages. There are plenty of products that boast "all natural ingredients" or that claim to be "natural" foods and drinks that simply aren't. In fact, most so-called natural foods you buy in stores that are labeled that way aren't good for you, and many of them are loaded with so much sugar, it's ridiculous that the companies that produce them can tell you they're healthy.

Remember this about food companies: the packaging on their products is meant to get you from the food aisle to the checkout counter with the product in your hand. They don't have any responsibility to you and your family. They don't care if their product is worsening your child's behavior problems. Looking at the ingredients list on the labels gives you the truest insight into what really *is* best for your child and your family to eat. As a rule of thumb, the fewer unnatural ingredients you find on the list, the better. (You've heard the saying, "If you haven't heard of it or can't pronounce it, it probably isn't good for you," right? It's true.) But also don't let yourself be fooled by clever euphemisms. Here are some lists to help you wade through the food aisles and emerge with things that are truly wholesome and good for your child.

First of all, avoid all foods with artificial food colors. Here are some of their common and uncommon names.

- Blue No. 1: can also be called Brilliant Blue FCF, E113
- Blue No. 2: can also be called Indigotine, E132
- Green No. 3: can also be called Fast Green FCF, E143
- Red No. 40: can also be called Allura Red AC, E129
- Red No. 3: can also be called Erythrosine, E127

- Yellow No. 5: can also be called Tartrazine, E102
- Yellow No. 6: can also be called Sunset Yellow FCF, E110

Avoid all foods with artificial sweeteners. Some artificial sweetener names can sound like names for vitamins, so this is tricky territory. Here is a list of words that should be regarded as red flags when you see them on an ingredients list:

- Acesulfame potassium (Acesulfame K)
- Alitame
- Aspartame
- Aspartame (Acesulfame-Salt)
- Cyclamate
- Dulcin
- Isomalt
- Neohesperidin dihydrochalcone
- Neotame
- P-4000
- Saccharin
- Sucralose

Avoid all foods with artificial flavorings. Note that companies are not required to list all the artificial flavorings they use (most don't have common names, anyway). They need only include the words "artificial flavors" in their ingredients list, so if you see it there, put down the box, the can, or the bottle. Some flavors deemed "natural flavors," such as almond flavor (benzaldehyde), are actually produced by the same companies, in the same factories, as artificial flavors and can similarly have adverse effects on behavior and mood in children with ADD/ADHD. If the label or package indicates "artificial flavors," "natural flavors added," "artificially sweetened," or even "naturally sweetened," "naturally flavored," or any flavors added at all, it's best to avoid these foods.

Don't take for granted that a package labeled "all natural" or "nutritious" is telling the truth and is good for you. Sugar, after all, is an all-natural food, but we all know by now just how unhealthy it is, especially for someone with ADD/ADHD.

Something I like to tell my patients and their parents is that my dog produces 100% natural, organic dog poop, but that doesn't mean we should be thinking about eating it. When you see "all natural" on a package, use your better judgment and turn the box, bag, or can over to check the ingredients.

When something is labeled as being vitamin fortified or "fortified with eleven vitamins and minerals," you have to ask, "Where did those original vitamins and minerals go?" They were processed out through bleaching and milling so much that they had to be added back in ways that still don't make them nearly as healthy as natural foods.

However, before you jump to the conclusion that at least some of their nutritive value has been restored, know that these nutrients have been added back in at unnatural ratios and quantities that are likely not right, not absorptive, not regulated by any government entity, and not healthy at all. "Enriched," "nutrient enriched," "fortified with vitamins and minerals," "vitamin-fortified," and the like are buzz words that should cause you to be suspicious that the foods they're describing aren't as natural or as healthy as the manufacturers' claim.

Shopping Substitutions

While you are at the grocery store, know that the ADD/ADHD cure is not all about limits. It is an opportunity to discover for yourself that certain everyday foods have better substitutes that are healthier and more nutritious. Processed food can be replaced with more natural options that your kids will enjoy just as much. Below is a chart that puts the bad alongside the good, and then the good alongside the better, for at-a-glance substitutions while shopping.

Bad	Good
Processed/refined sugar	Honey, grade B maple syrup, agave, molasses (in very limited amounts)
Cheese	Soy cheese
Milk	Soy milk
Candy	Nuts/seeds (in their shells, they're also fun to eat)

Bad	**Good**
Cookies/crackers/chips	Rice cakes/crackers
Canned vegetables	Fresh vegetables
White/wheat flour	Brown rice flour, bulgur, oat flour
Sugary boxed cereals	Bagged plain cereals (puffed corn, puffed rice, etc., with nothing added) or oatmeal
White bread	Pita and multigrain breads
Vegetable oil	Olive oil
Soda	Natural, unsweetened fruit juices
Good	**Better**
Fresh produce	Organic produce
Fresh organic, hormone-free meats/poultry	Tofu, fresh fish, or beans
Traditional whole-grain pastas	Gluten-free pastas
White rice	Brown, long-grain, and wild rice
Dried fruits	Fresh fruits

A Thirty-Day ADD/ADHD Cure Meal Plan

The following thirty-day meal plan fits all the requirements outlined in this chapter. Remember: it's not the end of the world if there is anything on the daily menus you and your kids won't like or that you don't want to or can't prepare. As long as you keep to the guidelines of the diet, you can feel free to improvise and add dishes to each meal or to replace them.

For example, soak any beans you want, run them through a blender, add any vegetables and spices you have handy, thin with water, and you now have a soup. Blend any fruits you have in the house with some ice for smoothies, or freeze them in frozen dessert trays, and you have a snack or an after-dinner dessert. Every meal can be complemented with a salad made with fresh ingredients. The possibilities are endless.

The meal plan here is for parents who prefer to follow a clear plan;

for those who'd like to add some delicious, healthful recipes to their knowledge base, or for those parents who would like a rough guide for reference when they run out of ideas.

Tip: If you plan to follow the meal plan day by day, check the next day's recipes the day before, in case there are any beans or grains that need to be soaked the night before, or something that can be done beforehand to save time the next day.

These kitchen tools are useful in preparing the meals in the plan:

- Blender and/or food processor
- Frozen dessert tray
- Vegetable steamer
- Cheese grater
- Wok and/or nonstick pan

The following chart outlines the thirty-day meal plan in detail. An asterisk indicates that the recipe is in this chapter.

WEEK 1

Monday

BREAKFAST	Hot Rice Cereal* and fresh fruit
LUNCH	Quesadillas* with Salsa* and Guacamole*
SNACK	Cut carrots with Guacamole*
DINNER	Hearty Stew* and mixed greens salad

Tuesday

BREAKFAST	Smoothie (there are several types of smoothies offered here for you to choose from)*
	Steel-Cut Oats* with raisins
LUNCH	Pita Pockets* and soy chips
SNACK	Hearty Stew*
DINNER	Mushroom Burgers,* Mashed Potatoes with Cauliflower and Gravy,* and mixed greens salad

Wednesday

BREAKFAST   Millet Cereal* and an apple or a pear

LUNCH   Baked soy pasta with leftover Mushroom Burgers* and Tomato Sauce*

SNACK   Cut-up vegetables with Green Goddess Dip*

DINNER   Carrot Soup,* Mexican Kidney Bean Salad,* and Stuffed Zucchini* with mushrooms, asparagus, and white beans

Thursday

BREAKFAST   Smoothie* and hot cereal

LUNCH   Leftover Mexican Kidney Bean Salad* and Carrot Soup*

SNACK   Corn Tortilla Snacks* with Salsa*

DINNER   Stir-Fry Vegetables with Brown Rice* and Mixed Vegetable Salad*

Friday

BREAKFAST   Smoothie* over a bowl of fresh fruit and cereal

LUNCH   Leftover Stir-fry Vegetables with Brown Rice*

SNACK   Tofu Sticks* with Tomato Sauce*

DINNER   Miso Soup,* Avocado and Rice Sushi,* and Japanese Salad*

Saturday

BREAKFAST   Pancakes from Scratch* with fresh fruit

LUNCH   Leftover Miso Soup* and Avocado and Rice Sushi*

SNACK   Cut-up vegetables with dip

DINNER   Tofu Lasagna* and mixed greens salad

Sunday

BREAKFAST   Smoothie* and Hot Rice Cereal*

LUNCH   Leftover Tofu Lasagna

SNACK   Corn Tortilla Snacks* with Salsa*

DINNER   Broccoli and Tofu with Mushroom Sauce,* baked yams, and mixed greens salad

WEEK 2

Monday

BREAKFAST   Cereal with fresh melon and soy milk

LUNCH   Quesadillas* made with baked yams

SNACK   Tofu Sticks* with Salsa*

DINNER   Mushroom and Vegetable Risotto* and mixed greens salad

Tuesday

BREAKFAST   Smoothie* and gluten-free toasted bread with apple butter

LUNCH   Avocado and Rice Sushi*

SNACK   Cut-up vegetables with dip

DINNER   Braised Tofu,* Mashed Potatoes with Cauliflower and Gravy,* and mixed greens salad

Wednesday

BREAKFAST   Hot cereal with soy milk and fruit

LUNCH   Soy Cheese Pizza* with vegetables

SNACK   Corn Tortilla Snacks* with Guacamole*

DINNER   Mexican platter (beans, rice, and chopped, grilled vegetables with Salsa* and Guacamole*)

Thursday

BREAKFAST   Hot cereal and Bananas in Fruit Sauce*

LUNCH   Tofu Sloppy Joes*

SNACK   Cut-up vegetables with dip

DINNER   Moroccan Vegetable Gumbo*

Friday

Breakfast	Hot cereal with soy milk and a banana
LUNCH	Pasta with Tomato Sauce*
SNACK	Cut-up melon and soy chips
DINNER	Grilled vegetables and potatoes over couscous with garbanzo beans and mixed greens salad

Saturday

BREAKFAST	Potato Pancakes* with apple butter and fresh berries
LUNCH	Leftover grilled vegetables and couscous
SNACK	Corn Tortilla Snacks* with Salsa*
DINNER	Tofu Lettuce Cups*

Sunday

BREAKFAST	Smoothie*
LUNCH	Black Bean Soup* with soy chips
SNACK	Fruit bowl with leftover Smoothie*
Dinner	Hearty Stew* and mixed greens salad

WEEK 3

Monday

BREAKFAST	Hot cereal with soy milk and fruit
LUNCH	Rice cracker sandwich with avocado, almond (or rice or soy) cheese, tomato, and lettuce
SNACK	Bean and rice soup with soy chips
DINNER	Vegetables with Tofu and Peanut Sauce,* rice, and mixed greens salad

Tuesday

BREAKFAST	Rice Cream Cereal* with fresh fruit
LUNCH	Leftover rice and Vegetables with Tofu and Peanut Sauce*

SNACK   Cut-up vegetables with Tofu Spread*

DINNER   Sweet-and-Sour Chinese Vegetables* and mixed greens salad

Wednesday

BREAKFAST   Steel-Cut Oats* with fresh berries

LUNCH   Pasta with Tomato Sauce*

SNACK   Seasonal fruit with chopped peanuts

DINNER   Stuffed Wontons,* leftover Sweet-and-Sour Chinese Vegetables,* and short-grain brown rice

Thursday

BREAKFAST   Millet Cereal* with soy milk and blueberries

LUNCH   Pita Pockets*

SNACK   Leftover Stuffed Wontons* fried lightly in canola oil (makes them crispy)

DINNER   Baked sweet potatoes, Broccoli and Cauliflower Sauté,* Braised Tofu,* and Three-Bean Salad*

Friday

BREAKFAST   Smoothie* and gluten-free toasted bread with fruit puree spread

LUNCH   Hearty Stew* with rice and soy chips

DINNER   Greek Potatoes* and mixed greens salad

Saturday

BREAKFAST   Pancakes from Scratch* with fresh fruit

LUNCH   Leftover Greek Potatoes* with rice

SNACK   Corn Tortilla Snacks* with Guacamole*

DINNER   Brown Rice and Mushroom Beignets* served over a salad, and sautéed carrots and celery with red onions

Sunday

BREAKFAST	Smoothie* and Hot Rice Cereal*
LUNCH	Corn tortilla sandwich with tomato, lettuce, shredded soy cheese, sliced olives, and Guacamole*
SNACK	Leftover Mushroom Beignets with Hummus*
DINNER	Burritos with Refried Beans,* sweet potatoes, and mixed greens salad

WEEK 4

Monday

BREAKFAST	Smoothie* and gluten-free toasted bread with apple butter
LUNCH	Sandwich of either tortillas, rice crackers, or gluten-free bread with tomato, grated soy cheese, and lettuce
SNACK	Cut-up vegetables with dip
DINNER	Vegetable Pilaf*

Tuesday

BREAKFAST	Hot cereal with soy milk and fresh berries
LUNCH	Soy noodles with tomato sauce
SNACK	Corn Tortilla Snacks* with Salsa*
DINNER	Tofu Lasagna*

Wednesday

BREAKFAST	Hot cereal with soy milk and bananas
LUNCH	Leftover Vegetable Pilaf*
SNACK	Sliced fruit with banana puree
DINNER	Quinoa with sautéed vegetables and tofu and mixed greens salad

Thursday

BREAKFAST	Pancakes from Scratch* with fresh fruit puree
LUNCH	Tofu Sloppy Joes* in corn tortillas
SNACK	Granola Bars* with fresh fruit
DINNER	Green Vegetable Risotto* and mixed greens salad

Friday

BREAKFAST	Hot cereal with soy milk and fresh fruit
LUNCH	Leftover Green Vegetable Risotto*
SNACK	Dollar-size pancakes with fruit puree
DINNER	Corn and Bean Nachos* and mixed greens salad

Saturday

BREAKFAST	Rice Cream Cereal* with fresh fruit
LUNCH	Corn tortillas stuffed with chopped vegetables and beans
SNACK	Rice crackers with tahini spread
DINNER	Winter Squash Stew* over short-grain brown rice, and mixed greens salad

Sunday

BREAKFAST	Multigrain waffles with soy whipped cream and berries
LUNCH	Tofu Sloppy Joes*
SNACK	Cut-up vegetables with dip
DINNER	(It's time to celebrate one month of good, healthy eating!) Soy Cheese Pizza* with toppings of your child's favorite vegetables and almonds or rice or any other combination, and tossed salad

Meal Plan Weekly Shopping Lists

The following shopping lists are for each of the four weeks of the ADD/ADHD Cure Thirty-Day Meal Plan. Please note that some of the ingredients (rice, spices, flour, oils, etc.) on the list for Week 1 are not repeated in Weeks 2 to 4 because you likely have enough left to last you after shopping the first week.

Make sure to supplement each list with an assortment of your kids' favorite fruits for them to grab as snacks and also to use as bagged salads to complement every meal.

Week 1 Shopping List

Fruits

- Apples or pears
- Blueberries
- Lemons
- Your favorite fruits and seasonal berries (for smoothies and purees)

Vegetables/Herbs

- Artichokes
- Avocados
- Basil
- Bay leaves
- Bok choy
- Broccoli
- Cabbage (red)
- Carrots
- Cauliflower
- Celery
- Chard (red or green)
- Cilantro
- Corn
- Cucumbers
- Dill
- Fennel or anise
- Garlic
- Lettuce (assorted, for salads)
- Mushrooms (button, Shitake, and white)
- Onions
- Parsley
- Peppers (red and green)
- Potatoes (white)
- Scallions (green onions)
- Serrano chilies
- Spinach
- Sweet potatoes
- Thyme
- Tomatoes
- Yams
- Yellow squash
- Zucchini

Beans/Rice/Grains/Nuts
- Adzuki beans
- Lentils
- Millet
- Quinoa
- Short-grain brown rice
- Steel-cut oats
- White beans
- Your favorite beans (for soups/stews)

Ready-Made
- Corn tortilla chips
- Corn tortillas
- Low-fat soy milk
- Nori seaweed
- Raisins
- Roasted beets
- Soy chips
- Soy mozzarella or almond cheese
- Soy pasta
- Tofu (extra firm, firm, and silken)
- Tomato paste
- Vanilla soy yogurt

Cooking/Baking
- Baking powder
- Bran flour
- Bread crumbs
- Cornmeal
- Dry sherry
- Flaxseeds (ground)
- Miso paste
- Oat flour
- Olive oil
- Peanut oil
- Red wine vinegar
- Rice flour
- Sesame oil

Seasonings/Spices
- Black pepper
- Cayenne pepper
- Chili flakes
- Cinnamon
- Cumin
- Dried dill
- Dried thyme
- Dry mustard
- Granulated garlic
- Honey
- Nutmeg
- Oregano
- Paprika
- Salt
- Soy sauce/tamari
- Turmeric
- White pepper

Week 2 Shopping List

Fruits

- Bananas
- Fresh melon (your choice)
- Strawberries or raspberries
- Your favorite fruits and seasonal berries (for smoothies and purees)

Vegetables/Herbs

- Basil
- Bay leaves
- Carrots
- Cauliflower
- Celery
- Cilantro
- Corn
- Dill
- Garlic
- Ginger
- Lettuce (assorted, for salads)
- Mushrooms
- Onions
- Peppers (red and green)
- Potatoes (white)
- Scallions (green onions)
- Serrano chilies
- Sweet potatoes
- Thyme
- Tomatoes
- Yams
- Zucchini

Beans/Rice/Grains/Nuts

- Beans (black and red)
- Couscous
- Garbanzo beans (chickpeas)

Ready-Made

- Apple butter
- Corn taco shells
- Corn tortillas
- Gluten-free bread
- Gluten-free pasta
- Raisins
- Soy chips
- Soy milk
- Tomato paste
- Tofu (extra firm and firm)
- Vanilla soy yogurt
- Water chestnuts

Cooking/Baking

- Cornstarch
- Dry yeast
- Multigrain or soy flour
- Vanilla

Seasonings/Spices
- Chili powder
- Coriander
- Saffron

Week 3 Shopping List

Fruits
- Blueberries
- Lemons
- Your favorite fruits and seasonal berries (for smoothies and purees)

Vegetables/Herbs
- Avocados
- Basil
- Bay leaves
- Broccoli
- Carrots
- Cauliflower
- Celery
- Chinese cabbage
- Cilantro
- Corn
- Garlic
- Ginger
- Lettuce (assorted, for salads)
- Mushrooms (button and white)
- Olives (black)
- Onions
- Parsley
- Peppers (red and green)
- Potatoes (white)
- Scallions (green onions)
- Serrano chilies
- Snow peas
- Sweet potatoes
- Tomatoes

Beans/Rice/Grains/Nuts
- Beans (black and pinto)
- Garbanzo beans (chickpeas)
- Millet
- Peanuts
- Sesame seeds
- Short-grain brown rice
- Steel-cut oats
- Yellow peas or red lentils
- Your favorite beans (for stews)

Ready-Made

- Corn tortilla chips
- Corn tortillas
- Extra-firm tofu
- Gluten-free bread
- Powdered soup stock
- Refried beans
- Soy cheese
- Soy milk
- Soy pasta
- Sweet-and-sour sauce
- Tahini
- Tomato paste
- Wonton wrappers

Cooking/Baking

- Baking powder
- Bread crumbs
- Canola oil
- Cornmeal
- Flour (bran, chickpea, oat, and rice)
- Miso paste
- Soy oil

Seasonings/Spices

- Chili flakes
- Chili powder
- Honey
- Molasses
- Soy sauce

Week 4 Shopping List

Fruits

- Bananas
- Figs or dates
- Your favorite fruits and berries (for smoothies and purees)

Vegetables/Herbs

- Asparagus
- Boy choy or white cabbage
- Broccoli
- Carrots
- Celery
- Chard (green or red)
- Cilantro
- Corn
- Garlic
- Ginger

- Hubbard squash
- Kabocha squash (or any winter squash)
- Lettuce (assorted, for salads)
- Onions
- Parsley
- Peas
- Peppers (green and red)
- Scallions (green onions)
- Serrano chilies
- Sweet potatoes
- Tomatoes
- White mushrooms
- Zucchini

Beans/Rice/Grains/Nuts

- Basmati rice
- Beans (red, navy, and white or fava)
- Cashews
- Long-grain white rice
- Pecans
- Quinoa
- Rolled oats
- Sesame seeds
- Short-grain brown rice

Ready-Made

- Apple butter
- Corn chips
- Corn tortillas
- Rice crackers or gluten-free bread
- Soy cheese (mozzarella) and/or almond cheese
- Soy milk
- Soy noodles
- Tahini
- Tofu (firm and extra-firm)
- Tomato paste
- Vanilla soy yogurt

Cooking/Baking

- Almond butter
- Brown rice flour
- Dry yeast
- Olive oil

Seasonings/Spices

- Maple syrup
- Marjoram

The ADD and ADHD Cure Recipes

Breakfast

HOT CEREALS

Hot Rice Cereal

½ cup short-grain brown rice, cooked
⅓ cup low-fat plain soy milk
Dash of cinnamon
Pinch of mace or nutmeg
1 tablespoon raisins

Combine all of the ingredients in a saucepan. Bring the mixture to a boil over medium-high heat. Cover and simmer over low heat for 5 to 10 minutes. Serve warm.

Rice Cream Cereal

2 cups cooked short-grain brown rice
1½ cups vanilla soy milk
1 tablespoon honey
2 teaspoons molasses
Dash of nutmeg
Dash of cinnamon

Place all of the ingredients in a blender or a food processor. Blend until smooth.

Pour the mixture into a saucepan. Bring to a boil over medium-high heat. Cover and simmer over low heat for 5 to 10 minutes. Serve warm.

Bananas and strawberries may also be added.

Steel-Cut Oats

This recipe is for one serving. Double or triple it if you want to make it for more people.

Unlike oatmeal, steel-cut oats are crunchy, and they supply more nutrition than oatmeal.

¼ cup steel-cut oats
½ cup water
1 tablespoon raisins

½ teaspoon cinnamon
2 tablespoon ground flaxseeds

Combine all of the ingredients in a small saucepan. Bring the mixture to a boil over medium-high heat. Lower the heat and let simmer for 5 minutes.
    Add a little soy milk before serving.

Millet Cereal

Prepare the millet ahead of time by pulverizing several cups of millet grain in a blender or a food processor. If you use a blender, pulverize small portions at a time. Store extra ground millet in a tightly covered container for later use.

½ cup pulverized millet
1 cup water
1 teaspoon raisins or blueberries

Combine all of the ingredients in a saucepan. Bring the mixture to a boil over medium-high heat. Lower the heat and let simmer for 5 minutes.
    Add a little soy milk before serving.

SMOOTHIES

As you read these recipes, you'll see that you can really do whatever you like. Buy fresh fruit that is currently in season. Wash, chop up, and package the fruit in small snack bags and freeze. In the frozen foods section of your market, there are many frozen fruits available if you want the added convenience. The frozen fruits thicken the smoothie and make it very tasty. Adding ice cubes also helps thicken smoothies.

Banana-Apple Smoothie

1 small banana
½ apple, peeled and sliced
½ cup plain soy yogurt
¼ cup orange juice or apple juice
½ cup frozen berries

Place all of the ingredients in a blender and blend until smooth—or chunky, if preferred.

Fresh Peach and Apple Smoothie

2 peaches, peeled and diced
1 bag frozen strawberries
½ cup plain soy yogurt
½ cup apple juice

Place all of the ingredients in a blender and blend until smooth.

Fresh Mixed-Berries Smoothie

2 snack bags of frozen berries
1 cup apple or orange juice
1 banana (optional)
½ cup plain soy yogurt (optional)

Place all of the ingredients in a blender and blend until smooth.

Blueberry and Apple Smoothie

1 snack bag frozen blueberries
½ cup orange juice
1 banana
1 small apple, peeled and sliced

Place all of the ingredients in a blender and blend until smooth.

Fresh Seasonal Melon Smoothie

1 cup diced honeydew or cantaloupe
½ cup plain soy yogurt
⅓ cup frozen blueberries
⅓ cup frozen strawberries

Place all of the ingredients in a blender and blend until smooth.

PANCAKES

There are many gluten-free flours and gluten-free pancake mixes available. There are different substitutes to use for eggs, including delicious vanilla soy yogurt. We have been off dairy for many years and find it easy and very tasty to use soy alternatives.

As a topping, use fresh or pureed berries and serve with sliced bananas.

Soy milk makes a wonderful "whipped cream."

Pancakes from Scratch

½ cup rice flour
¼ cup bran flour
¼ cup oat flour
2 tablespoons cornmeal
1 teaspoon baking powder
½ cup soy milk
1 tablespoon oil
2 tablespoons vanilla soy yogurt

Combine the rice flour, bran flour, oat flour, cornmeal, and baking powder in a medium bowl. In a separate bowl, combine the soy milk, oil, and soy yogurt.

Mix the liquid ingredients into the dry ingredients and stir until smooth.

Oil a griddle or a small nonstick frying pan and set it over medium heat. When the pan is hot, drop dollops of the batter into it. When small bubbles appear on top of the pancakes (2 to 3 minutes), flip them over and cook completely (another 2 to 3 minutes).

Crepes

½ cup rice flour
¼ cup bran flour
¼ cup oat flour
2 tablespoons cornmeal
1 teaspoon baking powder
½ cup soy milk
1 tablespoon oil
2 tablespoons vanilla soy yogurt
½ cup soy milk

Combine the rice flour, bran flour, oat flour, cornmeal, and baking powder in a medium bowl. In a separate bowl, combine the soy milk, oil, soy yogurt, and soy milk.

Mix the liquid ingredients into the dry ingredients and stir until smooth.

Oil a small nonstick frying pan and set it over medium heat. When the pan is hot, pour in batter thinner than you would for pancakes. Cook for about 3 minutes, then flip over the crepes and cook for just a few seconds more.

Tip: These are great served with berries and berry purees.

Dips and Spreads

Almost all bean spreads use cooked beans. It's a good idea to have cooked beans on hand, and they are easily frozen in small quantities.

Soak several cups of beans in a pot large enough to cover the beans with twice as much water. I recommend soaking beans overnight and cooking them the next day. When you are ready to cook the beans, bring a pot of water to a boil, add the beans, and simmer them for 1 to 2 hours, depending on the type of bean.

When the beans are soft (not mushy), fill containers with them, including some of the cooking liquid, and freeze what you aren't using immediately. This early preparation makes soups and stews much faster to cook.

Hummus

1 cup cooked garbanzo beans (chickpeas)
¼ cup lemon juice
2 garlic cloves, peeled and chopped
¼ cup tahini
½ cup olive oil
1 tablespoon soy sauce (or tamari)
Dash of chili powder (optional)

Place all of the ingredients in a food processor and pulse until smooth.

Green Hummus

1 cup cooked garbanzo beans (chickpeas)
1 cup chopped spinach
¼ cup fresh chopped parsley (or 2 tablespoons parsley flakes)
¼ cup lemon juice
2 garlic cloves, peeled and chopped
¼ cup tahini
½ cup olive oil
1 tablespoon soy sauce (or tamari)
Dash of chili powder (optional)

Place all of the ingredients in a food processor and pulse until smooth.

Red Hummus

1 cup cooked garbanzo beans (chickpeas)
½ cup diced tomatoes
2 tablespoons chopped fresh basil (or 1 tablespoon dried basil)
¼ cup lemon juice
2 garlic cloves, peeled and chopped
¼ cup tahini
½ cup olive oil
1 tablespoon soy sauce (or tamari)
Dash of chili powder (optional)

Place all of the ingredients in a food processor and pulse until smooth.

Olive Tapenade

2 tablespoons chopped white onion
½ pound kalamata olives, pitted
⅓ cup capers
2 tablespoons olive oil
1 tablespoon lemon juice (or balsamic vinegar)
Dash of ground pepper
Pinch of thyme
Pinch of dill

Place all of the ingredients in a food processor and pulse on and off for 30 seconds. The tapenade can be served chunky or smooth.

Baba Ghanoush

2 large or 4 small eggplants
2 tablespoons red wine vinegar
2 tablespoons olive oil
1 tablespoon chopped fresh parsley
Pinch of red chili flakes
Dash of salt
Dash of ground pepper

Preheat the oven to 400 degrees F.

Prick the eggplants with a fork and place them on an oiled baking sheet. Bake for 40 to 50 minutes until the eggplants are soft, depending on how round they are. The eggplants are done when the area around the stem is soft.

Remove the eggplants from the oven and let sit for 10 minutes. When the eggplants are cool enough to handle, scoop out the insides into the bowl of a food processor.

Add the remaining ingredients to the food processor and pulse on and off for 20 seconds.

Guacamole

1 large tomato, seeded and chopped
¼ cup chopped white onion
1 tablespoon chopped cilantro
3 tablespoons minced red bell pepper
3 large avocados, pitted
½ teaspoon chili flakes
1 small serrano chili pepper, diced (2 tablespoons if canned and chopped)
Pinch of salt
Dash of ground pepper

Combine all of the ingredients in a large bowl and mash to the desired consistency. Guacamole can be chunky or smooth.

Black Bean Dip

1 cup cooked black beans
½ cup tomato sauce or chopped fresh tomatoes
¼ cup chopped onion
¼ cup chopped red bell pepper
1 tablespoon dried cilantro flakes
Pinch of salt
Dash of ground pepper
1 cup cooked corn kernels

Place all of the ingredients except the corn kernels in a food processor and pulse until smooth. Scoop out the mixture into a bowl and stir in the corn.

Tofu Spread

Tofu Spread is great on sandwiches as a mayonnaise substitute.

1 pound extra-firm tofu, cubed
⅓ cup chopped green onions

1 tablespoon chopped fresh garlic (or ½ teaspoon granulated garlic)
½ teaspoon soy sauce
1 tablespoon miso paste
1 teaspoon lemon juice
½ cup olive oil
½ teaspoon dry mustard
½ teaspoon turmeric

Place all of the ingredients in a food processor and pulse until smooth.

Tomato Relish

Tomato Relish is similar to salsa and great with corn chips. It's also a great way to get protein.

2 large tomatoes, chopped
¼ cup chopped red bell pepper
¼ cup minced onion
¼ cup minced cilantro
⅓ cup balsamic vinegar
Pinch of parsley flakes
Pinch of red pepper flakes
Pinch of salt
Dash of ground pepper
1 cup cooked red beans

Combine all of the ingredients except the beans in a bowl, cover, and let marinate for several hours.

Stir in the beans.

Mushroom Caviar

2 tablespoons olive oil
1 small onion, chopped
2 garlic cloves, chopped
1 pound white mushrooms, sliced
1 tablespoon tamari
1 teaspoon dried thyme
Dash of pepper

Heat the olive oil in a skillet over medium-high heat. Sauté the onion and garlic until the onion is translucent, about 8 minutes. Add the mushrooms and continue sautéing for 4 minutes. Add the tamari. Stir to combine, then remove from the heat.

Place all of the cooked ingredients in a food processor. Add the thyme and pepper. Pulse on and off 5 times.

Dal (Lentil Dip)

Dal can be served chunky or smooth. Smooth dal makes a great side dish or an alternative to mayonnaise on a sandwich.

1 cup lentils
3 cups vegetable stock
1 cup chopped onion
2 garlic cloves, minced
1 teaspoon mustard seeds
2 tablespoons olive oil
2 tablespoons chopped red bell pepper
1 cup chopped tomato
½ teaspoon ground cumin
½ teaspoon ground coriander
½ teaspoon turmeric
1 teaspoon soy sauce

Combine the lentils and vegetable stock in a saucepan. Cook over low heat until the lentils are tender, about 20 minutes. Add a little water if the mixture begins to dry out.

Heat the olive oil in a skillet over medium-high heat. Sauté the onion, garlic, and mustard seeds until the onion is translucent, about 8 minutes. Add the red pepper and tomato and continue to sauté for 2 to 3 minutes.

Add all of the remaining ingredients to the skillet and stir to combine. If you prefer a chunky dal, serve the mixture now. If want a smoother dal, pour the mixture into the bowl of a food processor, allow to cool, and pulse a few times.

Green Goddess Dressing or Dip

1 pound silken or extra-firm tofu, cubed
1 cup chopped spinach
½ cup chopped parsley

2 garlic cloves, minced
½ cup water
¼ cup red wine vinegar
½ teaspoon dried dill
Pinch of salt
Dash of white pepper

Place all of the ingredients in a food processor and pulse for 10 seconds or until smooth for a dip or a spread.

If you're making this for a salad dressing, thin the mixture with a little olive oil.

Salsa

4 large tomatoes, chopped and seeded
1 bunch of green onions, chopped
4 garlic cloves, minced
1 cup loosely packed, chopped cilantro
½ cup minced green pepper (optional)
1 cup corn kernels (optional)
1 small serrano chili, minced (yields 2–3 tablespoons)
½ teaspoon ground cumin

Combine all of the ingredients in a nonmetal bowl. Mix well, cover, refrigerate, and allow to marinate for several hours.

For a sweet version of this salsa, add:

1 cup cubed pineapple
1 cup chopped papaya
1 cup apricot juice

Quick-Fix Lunches

All kids love sandwiches. Today, there are many varieties of not only sandwiches but also breads in different shapes, sizes, textures, and flavors. Search in your market or local health food store for gluten-free breads, corn tortillas, and "flours" for crepes.

Try the soy breads and rice wrappers found in the refrigerator section of your local markets. Following are ideas for sandwiches and quick lunches.

Corn Tortilla Snacks

Preheat the oven to 350 degrees F.

Cut the tortillas into 6 pieces each. Place the tortilla wedges onto an oiled baking sheet and heat in the oven for 3 to 5 minutes.

Serve hot with Guacamole (see page 64, or store-bought) and/or Salsa (see page 67, or store-bought).

Bean and Rice Burritos in Corn Tortillas

Preheat the oven to 350 degrees F.

Place a tortilla on an oiled baking sheet. Fill with rice and cooked beans and roll up. Top with salsa and shredded soy or almond cheese. Heat the tortilla in the oven for 3 to 5 minutes.

Quesadillas

Preheat the oven to 375 degrees F.

Place a corn tortilla on an oiled baking sheet and layer with cooked beans; sautéed onions, mushrooms, and peppers; shredded soy or almond cheese; cooked broccoli; or anything else you like. Top with another tortilla. Bake in the oven for 5 minutes. Serve with salsa.

Tip: Use leftovers and your imagination to create whatever you like. For instance, try filling the corn tortillas with mashed sweet potatoes and sautéed onions.

Burritos

Preheat the oven to 350 degrees F.

Place a corn tortilla onto an oiled baking sheet. Refer to the Quesadillas recipe above for filling ingredients. Rice and beans are your best vegan protein fillings. Add shredded soy cheese and sautéed onions for a great taste. Add your fillings and roll up the tortilla.

Pour tomato sauce (see the recipe for Pasta with Tomato Sauce on page 111) over the burrito and sprinkle with grated soy or almond cheese. Bake for 20 minutes.

Serve the burrito with Guacamole (see page 64, or store-bought) and/or Salsa (see page 67, or store-bought).

Tip: For a spicy tomato sauce, mince 1 serrano chili and add to the sauce. Simmer the sauce in a small saucepan for 5 minutes before pouring over the burrito.

Tofu Sticks

Slice a 1-pound package of extra-firm tofu into ¾-inch sticks.

Heat a small amount of olive oil in a skillet over medium-high heat. Place the tofu sticks into the hot pan.

Allow the tofu to brown slightly, about 2 minutes, then turn over the sticks carefully. Add a little more oil if necessary. Turn the sticks two more times until all sides are browned, about 2 minutes per side. Drizzle a little soy sauce onto the sticks and toss gently so they don't lose their shape. The tofu sticks can be serve hot or cold and with or without a dip. They keep well in a sealed container for several days.

Tofu sticks are a great filling for burritos and quesadillas, taste wonderful in soups and salads, and make a great side dish for a meal.

Sweet Potato Pancakes

2 cups mashed sweet potatoes (peeled or unpeeled)
½ cup oat flour, or enough to form a shape
½ teaspoon cinnamon

Combine all of the ingredients in a bowl. Heat a small amount of olive oil in a skillet over medium-high heat. Drop spoonfuls of the batter into the pan to form small pancakes. Brown the pancakes on one side, 3 to 4 minutes. Flip and brown the other side, another 3 to 4 minutes.

Serve with soy sour cream and/or applesauce.

Potato Pancakes

3 cups shredded unpeeled white potatoes
1 large onion, chopped and sautéed
¾–1 cup oat flour
½ cup plain soy yogurt

Combine all of the ingredients in a bowl. Heat a small amount of olive oil in a skillet over medium-high heat. Drop spoonfuls of the batter into the pan to form small pancakes. Brown the pancakes on one side, 3 to 4 minutes. Flip and brown the other side, another 3 to 4 minutes.

Serve with applesauce.

Brown Rice and Mushroom Pancakes or Beignets

2 cups cooked brown rice
½ cup minced onion
½ cup shredded carrots
2 garlic cloves, minced
½ cup minced and sautéed mushrooms
½ cup oat flour
1 teaspoon soy sauce

Combine all of the ingredients in a bowl. Heat a small amount of olive oil in a skillet over medium-high heat. Spoon out small rounds of dough into the pan. Brown the pancakes on one side, 3 to 4 minutes. Flip and brown the other side, another 3 to 4 minutes.

For beignets, shape the dough into balls and cook on all sides until brown, 4 to 5 minutes.

Chili with Tofu

2 small onions, chopped
3 garlic cloves, minced
1 or 2 small serrano chilies, seeded and minced
½ cup diced green bell pepper
3 tablespoons olive oil
1 pound tempeh or extra-firm tofu, crumbled
2–3 cups cooked kidney beans
2 cups tomato sauce (see the recipe for Pasta with Tomato Sauce on
    page 111)
2 tablespoons chili powder
1 tablespoon soy sauce
1 teaspoon cumin

Heat a small amount of olive oil in a skillet over medium-high heat. Sauté the onions and garlic until the onion is translucent, about 8 minutes. Add the chilies and green pepper. Stir in the olive oil and tempeh. Mix well. Add the beans, tomato sauce, chili powder, soy sauce, and cumin.

Cover, reduce the heat to low, stirring often, and simmer for 30 minutes.

Pita Pockets

½ cup chopped green onions
2 garlic cloves, minced
2 cups mashed cooked garbanzo beans (chickpeas)
1 cup cooked yellow peas or red lentils
1½ cups oat flour
1 cup cornmeal
½–1 cup chickpea flour
2 tablespoons olive oil
Shredded lettuce
1 tomato, chopped, or Salsa (see page 67, or store-bought)
Hummus or tahini

Heat a small amount of olive oil in a skillet over medium-high heat. Sauté the onion and garlic until the onion is translucent, about 8 minutes. Transfer the onion and garlic to a bowl. Add the garbanzo beans, yellow peas, and ½ cup of the oat flour. Mix well. The mixture should be able to be formed into a ball. Add more flour if needed.

In a separate bowl, combine the remaining cup oat flour with the cornmeal and chickpea flour.

Heat the olive oil in a skillet over medium-high heat. Using a tablespoon of the chickpea dough at a time, roll the dough into balls (falafels). Coat the falafels with the flour mixture. Fry the falafels in the skillet, turning often but gently, for about 5 minutes or until brown.

Remove the falafels from the skillet with a slotted spoon. Place on a paper towel to drain the excess oil.

To form sandwiches, hold an opened pita pocket in one hand. Spoon in shredded lettuce, three falafels, and chopped tomatoes or salsa, and top with hummus or tahini.

Mushroom Burgers

1 cup mixed dried, wild mushrooms (these come packed in the produce
    sections of markets)
2 small white onions, minced
4 cloves garlic, minced
3 tablespoons olive oil
1 bunch green onions, chopped
2 cups sliced white mushrooms

1 cup grated carrots
1 cup minced celery
½ cup minced red bell pepper
2 cup cooked lentils
1 cup oat flour

In a bowl, soak the dried mushrooms in water for 20 minutes. Drain the mushrooms, cut off the stems, and chop.

Preheat the oven to 350 degrees F.

Heat the olive oil in a skillet over medium-high heat. Sauté the onions and garlic until the onions are translucent, about 8 minutes. Add the dried mushrooms, white mushrooms, carrots, celery, and red pepper. Continue to sauté until the carrots are soft, about 5 minutes Transfer the mixture to a bowl. Stir in the lentils and oat flour. Mix well.

Form the mixture into patties and place in a nonstick baking dish. Bake in the oven for about 20 minutes or until the patties are cooked through.

The mushroom burgers will keep for one day in the refrigerator.

Tip: These burgers can be crumbled into tomato sauce or made into small "meatballs."

Tofu Sloppy Joes

3 tablespoons olive oil
1 small white onion, minced
2 cloves garlic, minced
½ pound extra-firm tofu, crumbled
½ cup minced red bell pepper
2 cups cooked red beans, mashed slightly
1½ cups tomato sauce (see the recipe for Pasta with Tomato Sauce on
   page 111)
1 tablespoon chili powder
1 teaspoon cumin

Heat the olive oil in a skillet over medium-high heat. Sauté the onion and garlic until the onion is translucent, about 8 minutes. Add the tofu, red pepper, and beans. Cook for 4 to 5 minutes. Stir in the tomato sauce, chili powder, and cumin. Cover, reduce the heat to medium, and simmer until heated through, about 10 minutes.

Serve the hot mixture stuffed into corn taco shells.

Salads and Dressings

SALADS

Salads make great lunches and they're a great addition to any dinner table. As long as you have frozen cooked beans and rice or quinoa (a wonderful grain from South America that is very easy and fast to cook) on hand, you can add any combination of fresh-cut vegetables and toss everything together. As you experiment, mix and match ingredients. Kids have favorites, so introduce different salads and see what works best for your family.

Asian Tofu Salad

1 pound extra-firm tofu, cut into small cubes
½ cup julienned green bell pepper
⅓ cup chopped green onion
1 cup mung bean sprouts
1½ cups shredded Chinese cabbage
1 cup shredded romaine lettuce
1 cup shredded carrots
2 tablespoons peanut oil
1 tablespoon toasted sesame oil
1 tablespoon soy sauce
⅓ cup rice vinegar
⅓ cup toasted sesame seeds

Combine the tofu, pepper, onion, bean sprouts, cabbage, lettuce, and carrots in a large bowl. Mix well. In a small bowl, whisk together the oils, soy sauce, and vinegar.

Pour the dressing over the tofu-vegetable mixture and toss gently. Top with the sesame seeds.

Mexican Kidney Bean Salad

1 cup cooked kidney beans
1 cup grated carrots
1 cup chopped celery
⅔ cup chopped red onion
1 cup seeded and chopped tomato

½ cup chopped red bell pepper
1 cup cooked corn kernels
½ cup cubed avocado
¼ cup chopped cilantro
3 tablespoons olive oil
⅓ cup red wine vinegar
1 tablespoon granulated garlic
1 teaspoon cumin
Pinch of salt
Dash of ground pepper

Combine the beans, carrots, celery, onion, tomatoes, red pepper, corn, avocado, and cilantro in a large bowl. Toss gently to mix.

In a small bowl, whisk together the olive oil, vinegar, garlic, cumin, salt, and pepper. Pour the dressing over the salad and toss gently.

Serve as a side dish or on a bed of shredded lettuce.

Indian-Flavored Salad

1 cup cooked garbanzo beans (chickpeas)
1 cup cauliflower florets, raw
1 cup cooked unpeeled white potato, diced into ¼-inch pieces
1 cup chopped celery
½ cup chopped onion
½ cup seeded and chopped tomatoes
1 tablespoon curry powder
2 tablespoons olive oil
1 tablespoon peanut oil
⅓ cup balsamic vinegar
1 teaspoon granulated garlic
1 teaspoon cumin
½ teaspoon turmeric
½ teaspoon cinnamon
½ cup roasted cashews
2–3 cups cooked basmati rice (white or brown)

Combine the garbanzo beans, cauliflower, potato, celery, onion, tomatoes, and curry powder in a large bowl. Toss gently to mix.

In a small bowl, whisk together the olive oil, peanut oil, vinegar, garlic, cumin, turmeric, and cinnamon. Pour the dressing over the salad and toss gently. Stir in the cashews and rice. Mix well.

Japanese Salad

½ cup sesame seeds
2 cups golden or red beets
2 cups cooked adzuki beans
2 cups chopped or shredded bok choy
1 cup shredded red cabbage
1 cup julienned zucchini (cut in 2-inch strips)
1 cup julienned carrots
½ cup shitake mushrooms
1 tablespoon sesame oil
2 tablespoons olive oil
1 tablespoon peanut oil
⅓ cup rice vinegar

Preheat the oven to 400 degrees F.

Sauté the sesame seeds in a skillet over high heat dry until brown, 3 to 4 minutes. Set aside.

Clean the beets well. Place the beets on a roasting pan and roast in the oven for 20 minutes. Remove the beets from the oven and cool. When they are cool, cut into cubes.

Combine the beans, bok choy, cabbage, zucchini, carrots, and mushrooms in a large bowl. Add the beet cubes. Mix well.

In a small bowl, whisk together the olive oil, peanut oil, and vinegar. Pour the dressing over the salad and toss gently. Sprinkle the sesame seeds on top of the salad.

Mixed Vegetable Salad

1 cup grated carrots
1 cup chopped celery
1 cup chopped broccoli
1 cup diced zucchini or yellow squash
½ cup grated Jerusalem artichoke
1 cup sliced white mushrooms
1 cup chopped red cabbage
1 fennel or anise bulb, sliced thinly
2 tablespoons olive oil
⅓ cup raspberry vinegar
1 cup grated beets
½ cup marinated artichoke hearts

Combine the carrots, celery, broccoli, squash, artichoke, mushrooms, cabbage, and fennel in a large bowl. Toss well.

In a small bowl, whisk together the olive oil and the vinegar. Pour the dressing over the salad and toss gently. Top with the beets and the artichoke hearts.

Serve on a bed of arugula or spinach leaves.

Three-Bean Salad

1 cup cooked kidney beans
1 cup cooked navy beans
½ cup cooked garbanzo beans (chickpeas)
1 cup grated carrots
1 cup chopped celery
¼ cup chopped green onion
½ cup chopped white onion
¼ cup chopped green bell pepper
¼ cup chopped parsley
1 tablespoon chopped fresh basil (optional)
3 tablespoons olive oil
⅓ cup white wine vinegar (or balsamic vinegar)
1 tablespoon granulated garlic
1 teaspoon dried dill
Pinch of salt
Dash of ground pepper

Combine the kidney beans, navy beans, garbanzo beans, carrots, celery, onions, green pepper, parsley, and basil in a large bowl. Toss well.

In a small bowl, whisk together the olive oil, vinegar, garlic, dill, salt, and pepper. Pour the dressing over the salad and toss gently.

Serve as a complete dish or on a bed of mixed baby lettuce.

Cooked Lentil Salad

2 cups cooked green lentils, chilled
½ cup chopped green onions
1 cup chopped celery
½ cup minced carrots
3 tablespoons olive oil
⅓ cup balsamic vinegar
2 garlic cloves, minced
½ teaspoon marjoram

½ teaspoon thyme
Dash of white pepper
½ cup sliced hearts of palm
1 small bunch parsley, chopped

Combine the lentils, onions, celery, and carrots in a large bowl. Toss well. In a small bowl, whisk together the oil, vinegar, garlic, marjoram, thyme, and pepper. Pour the dressing over the salad and toss gently.

To serve, spoon on a bed of lettuce and top with the hearts of palm and the parsley.

Roasted Vegetable Salad

Baby squashes
Beets
Carrots
Parsnips
Pearl onions
Rutabaga
Sweet potatoes or yams
Turnips

Sprig of rosemary
Sprig of thyme

Preheat the oven to 350 degrees F.

Wash, peel, and slice the vegetables. Place the vegetables on a roasting pan with the sprigs of rosemary and thyme. Toss with a little olive oil or mist with an oil spray.

Roast the vegetables in the oven for 40 minutes, turning them every 10 minutes.

This salad can be served hot or cold.

VARIATIONS

1. If serving cold, toss the vegetables with:
   3 tablespoons olive oil
   ⅓ cup champagne vinegar or lemon juice
   Pinch of salt
   Dash of ground pepper

2. If serving hot, place the vegetables on a bed of lettuce with tahini sauce.

Steamed Vegetable Salad

2 cups chopped carrots
2 cups chopped celery
1 cup pearl onions
¼ cup chopped red bell pepper
1 cup broccoli florets
1 cup cauliflower florets
1 cup diced white potato (¼-inch cubes)
⅓ cup olive oil
⅓ cup raspberry vinegar
¼ cup chopped parsley
1 tablespoon granulated garlic
1 teaspoon dried dill
Pinch of salt
Dash of ground pepper

Add enough water to a large stockpot to cover the carrots, celery, onions, pepper, broccoli, cauliflower, and potato. Steam until the vegetables are tender, about 12 minutes. Transfer the steamed vegetables to a large bowl to cool.

In a small bowl, whisk together the oil, vinegar, parsley, garlic, dill, salt, and pepper. Pour the dressing over the vegetables and toss gently.

Serve the vegetables on a bed of romaine lettuce.

Avocado and Tofu Salad

1 cup firm tofu, cut into ¼-inch cubes
1 cup chopped celery
¼ cup chopped green onion
¼ cup chopped red bell pepper
Spinach leaves (or any other lettuce you prefer)
1 cup grated carrots
½ avocado, sliced
2 tablespoons sunflower seeds or raisins

Combine the tofu, celery, onion, and red pepper in a medium bowl. Toss gently.

Arrange the spinach leaves to lay flat on a serving platter. Spoon the tofu mixture on the spinach leaves to form a nest. Put the carrots in the center. Arrange the avocado slices around the center.

Pour any dressing you like over the salad. Top with the sunflower seeds.

Caesar Salad with Croutons

1 slice gluten-free bread
1 bunch chilled romaine lettuce leaves, torn into bite-size pieces
⅓ cup Caesar Dressing (see page 83)
2 tablespoons grated soy cheese

Toast the bread and let it stand for 10 minutes, then cut it into cubes.

Gently toss the lettuce with the dressing in a large bowl. Add the croutons and the soy cheese.

Corn and Bean Salad

1 cup cooked black beans
1 cup cooked corn kernels
¼ cup chopped red pepper
¼ cup chopped green pepper
½ cup grated carrots
½ cup chopped celery
¼ cup chopped green onion
⅓ cup balsamic vinegar
2 cloves garlic, chopped
¼ cup chopped parsley
1 tablespoon dill
½ teaspoon soy sauce
Romaine lettuce leaves

Combine the beans, corn, peppers, carrots, celery, and onion in a large bowl. Toss gently.

In a small bowl, whisk together the vinegar, garlic, parsley, dill, and soy sauce. Pour the dressing over the vegetables and toss gently.

Arrange the romaine lettuce on a plate to form a nest. Spoon the salad on top of the lettuce. Serve chilled.

Marinated Bean Salad

1 cup red wine vinegar
½ cup apple cider vinegar
1–2 tablespoons tamari or soy sauce
⅓ cup water
1 bay leaf
1 teaspoon dried dill
¼ teaspoon white ground pepper

1 cup chopped celery
½ cup minced onion
1 tablespoon chopped garlic
½ cup cooked kidney beans
½ cup cooked garbanzo beans (chickpeas)
½ cup cooked navy beans
½ cup cooked pinto beans

In a large bowl, whisk together all of the ingredients except the beans. Pour the marinade over the beans. Toss gently before covering and refrigerating the bean marinade overnight. Mix the beans every few hours to make sure they are marinated evenly.

VARIATIONS

1. Serve the marinated beans on a tossed salad of mixed baby greens.
2. Mix grated carrots and zucchini into the beans for a side dish.
3. Mash the beans and serve on a piece of toast for a light lunch or a quick snack.

Oriental Tofu Salad

1-pound block of tofu, cut into ¼-inch cubes
½ cup chopped green bell pepper
½ cup chopped green onions
1½ cups mung bean sprouts
1½ cups shredded Chinese cabbage
1 cup shredded romaine lettuce
1 cup shredded carrots
Asian Dressing (see page 85)
2 tablespoons toasted sesame seeds

Combine all of the ingredients except the dressing and sesame seeds in a large bowl. Pour the dressing over the salad and toss gently. Top with the sesame seeds. Serve chilled.

Purple Cabbage Salad

2 cups shredded purple cabbage
1 cup shredded Chinese cabbage
¼ cup thinly sliced radish
¼ cup chopped green onion

2 cups shredded romaine lettuce
1 cup grated carrots
½ cup corn kernels
Spicy Vinegar Dressing (see page 85)

Combine all of the ingredients except the dressing in a large bowl. Pour the dressing over the salad and toss gently.

Rice and Bean Salad

1 cup cooked kidney beans
1 cup cooked black beans
1 cup cooked soybeans
1½ cups cooked short-grain brown rice
½ cup cooked wild rice
1 cup chopped celery
1 small onion, chopped
1 cup shredded carrots
Large leaf of romaine lettuce
½ cup mung beans

Combine the beans, brown rice, wild rice, celery, onion, and carrots in a large bowl. Gently toss the salad with your favorite dressing and serve on a large leaf of romaine lettuce. Garnish the salad with the mung beans.

Tabouleh

1 cup water
Dash of salt
1 cup dry bulgur wheat
½ cup chopped parsley
¼ cup chopped mint
1 cup diced tomato
¼ cup lemon juice
Pinch of salt
Dash of ground pepper
Vegetables (your choice)

Add the water and salt to a large pot and bring to a boil over high heat. Add the bulgur wheat to the pot and cover. Turn off the heat and let stand covered for 15 to 20 minutes. Remove from the heat, place in a covered container, and let the bulgur cool in the refrigerator.

Combine the parsley, mint, tomatoes, lemon juice, salt, and pepper in a large bowl.

Toss in the cooled bulgur wheat. You can add your favorite vegetables, such as grated carrots, diced broccoli, cucumbers, peppers, cauliflower, or celery.

Tomato and Bean Salad

2 large tomatoes, sliced ¼ inch thick
1 cup shredded soy cheese
1 cup marinated beans (see the recipe for Marinated Bean Salad on
    page 79)
4 tablespoons chopped parsley

Set the oven to broil.

On a baking sheet lined with parchment paper, lay out the tomato slices. Top with the cheese and broil for 6 to 8 minutes or until the cheese melts. Remove the tomatoes from the broiler.

On four separate plates, place two tomato slices side by side. Top with the marinated beans and chopped parsley.

Tossed Spinach Salad

1 bunch of spinach leaves, torn into bite-size pieces
1 small head of butter lettuce leaves, torn into bite-size pieces
1 cup chopped celery
¼ cup chopped yellow pepper
¾ cup sliced mushrooms
Mustard Vinaigrette (see page 84) or Lemon Dill Dressing (see page 84)
½ cup alfalfa sprouts

Combine the spinach, lettuce leaves, celery, yellow pepper, and mushrooms in a large bowl. Pour the dressing over the salad and toss gently. Top with the alfalfa sprouts.

DRESSINGS

All of these dressings will keep in a sealed container in the refrigerator for two to four days.

Caesar Dressing

2 teaspoons olive oil
2 cloves garlic, crushed
¼ cup lemon juice
1 tablespoon soy sauce
2 tablespoon soy milk

Place all of the ingredients in a jar, cover, and shake well.

Creamy Herb Dressing

½ cup Tofu Mayonnaise (see page 86)
¼ cup red wine vinegar
1 teaspoon dried dill
1 garlic clove, minced
1 teaspoon prepared mustard
Dash of black pepper

Place all of the ingredients in a blender and blend until well combined.

Cucumber Dressing

1 cup red wine vinegar
¼ cup water
2 tablespoons honey
3 tablespoons lemon juice
½ teaspoon soy sauce
Dash of powdered mustard
½ teaspoon basil
3 cucumbers, peeled and diced
2 tomatoes, seeded and chopped

Mix all of the ingredients except the cucumbers and tomatoes in a large bowl until well combined. Add the cucumbers, cover, and allow to marinate overnight in the refrigerator.

Place the cucumber marinade and tomatoes in a blender and blend until well combined.

Dijon Mustard Dressing

½ cup Tofu Mayonnaise (see page 86)
1 tablespoon olive oil
¼ cup lemon juice

¼ cup Dijon mustard
Juice from 2 garlic cloves
1 teaspoon dried dill
Dash of pepper

Place all of the ingredients in a blender and blend until well combined.

French Herb Dressing

½ cup Tofu Mayonnaise (see page 86)
¼ cup lemon juice
1 garlic clove, minced
1 tablespoon dried dill
2 tablespoon dried parsley
½ teaspoon thyme

Place all of the ingredients in a blender and blend until well combined.

Japanese Radish Dressing

1 medium (8-inch) daikon (Japanese radish)
1 small onion, cut into pieces
2 teaspoons soy sauce
2 tablespoons rice vinegar
4 tablespoons water
2 tablespoons safflower oil

Place all of the ingredients in a blender and blend until smooth.

Lemon Dill Dressing

½ cup lemon juice
2 tablespoons olive oil
2 tablespoons water
⅛ teaspoon soy sauce
1 teaspoon granulated garlic or 1 garlic clove, minced
1 tablespoon dried dill

Place all of the ingredients in a blender and blend for 30 seconds.

Mustard Vinaigrette

½ cup white wine vinegar
1 tablespoon canola oil
1 tablespoon olive oil

2 tablespoons lemon juice
1 tablespoon prepared mustard
1 teaspoon dried dill
2 tablespoons water
1 tablespoon honey

Place all of the ingredients in a blender and blend for 30 seconds.

Asian Dressing

1 tablespoon canola oil
1 tablespoon sesame oil
2 tablespoons rice vinegar
1 tablespoon soy sauce
1 garlic clove, crushed
1-inch slice of ginger
1 teaspoon miso paste
Dash of cayenne pepper

Place all of the ingredients in a jar, cover, and shake well. Remove the ginger slice before serving.

Sesame Vinaigrette

1 teaspoon sesame oil
1 teaspoon soybean oil
4 tablespoons rice vinegar
1 tablespoon honey
¼ cup water
Dash of cayenne pepper
Dash of soy sauce

Place all of the ingredients in a blender and blend until well combined.

Spicy Vinegar Dressing

½ cup red wine vinegar
2 tablespoons olive oil
⅛ teaspoon cayenne pepper
⅛ teaspoon dried basil leaves
1 garlic clove, crushed
⅛ teaspoon soy sauce

Place all of the ingredients in a blender and blend until well combined.

Summer Fresh Dressing

½ cup orange juice
⅓ cup balsamic vinegar
1 cup olive oil
½ teaspoon dried basil leaves
½ teaspoon soy sauce
Dash of ground pepper

Place all of the ingredients in a jar, cover, and shake well.

Tofu Mayonnaise

This spread makes a wonderful base for creamy salad dressings.

1 pound firm tofu, cubed
3 tablespoon lemon juice
⅓ cup water
1½ tablespoons canola oil
1½ tablespoons miso paste
1 teaspoon tamari or soy sauce

Place all of the ingredients in a blender and blend until smooth. Add
more water slowly if you want a thinner consistency.

Vinaigrette

¼ cup orange juice
1 teaspoon orange peel, minced
3 tablespoons brown rice vinegar
3 tablespoons safflower oil
1 teaspoon soy sauce
¼ teaspoon ginger juice or 3 very thin slices of fresh ginger
1 garlic clove, minced

Place all of the ingredients in a blender and blend until smooth.

Soups

Make large amounts of soup and freeze some in smaller containers for
lunch or snacks, or puree and use as a sauce over rice and vegetables.
This saves countless hours of cooking, not to mention having to come up
with an idea for dinner or an afternoon snack.

Basic Soup Stock

4 large carrots, cut into large chunks and discard the ends
1 small whole stalk of celery, leaves and all, cut into large pieces
3 onions, cut into large pieces
10 mushrooms, cut in half
1 parsnip, discard the ends
$\frac{1}{2}$ tablespoon pepper
1 tablespoon soy sauce
8 garlic cloves, peeled and cut in half
1 bunch parsley
1 sprig dill
3 bay leaves

Place the carrots, celery, onions, mushrooms, parsnip, pepper, and soy sauce in a large soup pot. Fill the pot with enough water to cover the vegetables. Place the pot on the stove over medium heat.

Lay the garlic, parsley, dill, and bay leaves on a piece of cheesecloth. Wrap the cloth around the herbs and tie in a bundle with a piece of clean string. Add the herb sachet to the pot.

Bring the stock to a boil and simmer until half the liquid is gone, 1 to 2 hours. Allow the stock to cool, then remove the parsnip and herb sachet from the pot and discard. Puree the stock in small batches in a blender. Pour into covered containers and freeze until needed.

The stock can be used in soups or as a broth with tofu and vegetable pieces.

Tomato Soup

6 cups chopped tomatoes
1 tablespoon granulated garlic
2 cups vegetable stock
1 teaspoon miso paste
$\frac{1}{2}$ teaspoon dried dill
$\frac{1}{2}$ teaspoon dried basil leaves
1 bay leaf
Croutons (optional)
Herbs (your choice; optional)

Place all of the ingredients except the croutons and optional herbs in a soup pot. Bring to a boil. Reduce the heat to low and simmer for 45 minutes, uncovered. Remove from the heat and allow to cool. Once cooled, puree the soup in small batches in a blender, if desired.

Add a little soy milk if you want to make cream of tomato soup. Garnish with croutons and an herb mix of your choice such as parsley, chopped spinach, and scallions.

Hearty Tomato Soup

2 tablespoons olive oil
2 onions, minced
2 garlic cloves, chopped
½ cup minced carrots
½ cup minced celery
3 8-oz cans organic tomato sauce*
1 tablespoon dried basil (or ⅓ cup fresh basil)
¼ cup dried soup stock (or 1 cup ready made)
2 bay leaves
1 teaspoon dried oregano
1½ cups cooked navy beans

Heat the olive oil in a skillet over medium-high heat. Sauté the onions, garlic, carrots, and celery until the onions are translucent, about 8 minutes. Transfer the vegetables to a soup pot and add the tomato sauce, basil, stock, bay leaves, and oregano. Stir and bring to a boil, then lower the heat, cover, and simmer for 45 minutes. Add the navy beans.

If the soup is too thick, add some water or toss in 1 cup chopped tomatoes and allow to simmer for another 15 minutes.

*You can use 8 cups of fresh tomatoes instead of tomato sauce. Bring a pot of water to a boil and add the tomatoes. Boil them for a few minutes, then drain them into a colander. Soak the tomatoes in cold water until they are cool enough for you to handle. Peel off the skin, then slice and seed the tomatoes before you chop them.

Vegetable Soup

There are many variations on the basic vegetable soup recipe. It's a good idea to start with onions, garlic, carrots, celery, and parsnip, and then add your favorite seasonal vegetables. Here is a sample of a basic soup. Add your choices, always remembering to pour in more liquid (water or stock) as needed and to adjust the seasonings to your taste.

2 large onions, chopped
4 carrots, chopped
6 celery stalks or one small bunch, chopped
1 parsnip, whole
4 tomatoes, chopped
½ cup chopped green peppers
2 tablespoons soy sauce
1 bay leaf
¼ teaspoon ground white pepper
1 teaspoon dried basil
1 cup chopped zucchini
1 cup chopped sweet potato
1 cup chopped russet or Idaho potato

Place all of the ingredients in a 6-quart pot. Add water, filling the pot to at least 2 inches above the vegetables. Bring to a boil, then reduce the heat and simmer for 1½ hours until the vegetables are tender. Remove the parsnip. Taste the soup and adjust the seasonings if necessary.

If you like a thick soup, puree some vegetables in a blender and pour the mixture into the pot. Thick vegetable soup also makes a great sauce for Green Vegetable Risotto (see page 102).

Black Bean Soup

2 large white onions, chopped
2 cups chopped celery
2 cups chopped carrots
2 cups chopped sweet potatoes
2 cups chopped and seeded tomatoes
16 cups water
½ cup powdered soup stock or 2 cups Basic Soup Stock (see page 87)
1 teaspoon dried basil leaves
1 teaspoon dried oregano
1 teaspoon dried dill
1 teaspoon garlic powder
2 cups cooked black beans

Place all of the ingredients except the beans in a large pot. Add water to cover the beans and place the pot over medium-high heat. Bring to a boil, then reduce the heat to low, cover the pot, and simmer for 30 minutes. Add the black beans. Re-cover and simmer for 1 hour.

Remove the soup from the heat and allow to cool. Place 1 cup of soup in a blender and puree until smooth. Add back to the soup to thicken. If you want a smoother consistency, puree more of the soup.

Split Pea Soup

2 cups chopped onions
1 cup chopped carrots
1 cup chopped celery
1 cup chopped tomato, seeded
1 whole parsnip
1 cup chopped white potato (unpeeled)
3 cups split green peas
16–18 cups water
2 teaspoons dried dill weed
1 tablespoon granulated garlic
2 tablespoons soy sauce (tamari preferred)
½ teaspoon white pepper

Place all of the ingredients in a large pot. Bring to a boil, then cover the pot, reduce the heat to low, and simmer for 1 hour, or until the ingredients are soft. Add more water if necessary. You want enough water to keep the vegetables from drying out, because pea soup will thicken naturally.

Remove the pot from the heat and allow the soup to cool. Remove and discard the parsnip. Puree the soup in a blender 1 cup at a time. You don't need to puree the entire batch. The peas will soften, further thickening the soup, so just puree enough soup until the desired consistency is reached.

Navy Bean and Pasta Soup

3 cups navy beans (soaked but uncooked)
1 cup chopped carrot
1 cup chopped celery
1 cup chopped onion
1 cup chopped sweet potato
2 cups water
⅓ cup powdered stock or 2 cups Basic Soup Stock (see page 87)
1 teaspoon granulated garlic
½ teaspoon dried dill

½ cup dry sherry
1–2 cups cooked soy or rice pasta tubes or fusilli
Fresh basil or dill, chopped (optional)

Place the beans in a large pot, add water, and bring to a boil. Reduce the heat to low. Add the carrots, celery, onion, sweet potato, water, stock, garlic, and dried dill.

In a small saucepan, boil and reduce the sherry by half, about 5 minutes. Add the reduced sherry to the soup.

Cover the pot and simmer the soup for 1 to 2 hours, adding hot water if the level gets too low. Add the cooked pasta to the soup and mix well.

Remove from the heat and garnish with the basil or fresh dill.

Hearty Stew

Any bean soup can be pureed in a blender and used as a base for stews. You can mix things up a bit by using black bean soup puree for a garbanzo stew.

Select your favorite vegetables, cut them into chunks, and cover with the stock or soup puree. Add water if you don't have enough stock to completely cover the vegetables.

In a skillet, sauté tofu or tempeh (chicken or shrimp) and add to the stew.

If you're adding chunks of broccoli, cook the broccoli first and add it toward the end of the cooking time so it doesn't get mushy.

Some suggested combinations are:

1. Carrots, celery, onion, cauliflower, cooked kidney beans, and chopped chard served with basmati rice

2. Cooked garbanzo beans (chickpeas), sautéed mushrooms in garlic, tomatoes, carrots, celery, and chunks of sweet potatoes and onions

3. Chopped and sautéed onions, mushrooms, and celery added to 1 cup tomato sauce with chunks of potatoes, chopped cilantro, ¼ cup chopped poblano chilies, and dashes of cumin, coriander, and garlic

Lentil Soup

Lentils do not need to be soaked first, so this is an easy last-minute soup to make.

10 cups water
2 large carrots, chopped
4 stalks celery, chopped
2 medium onions, chopped
2 medium sweet potatoes, chopped
2 cups green lentils
½ cup powdered stock or 1 cup Basic Soup Stock (see page 87)
1 tablespoon granulated garlic
1 teaspoon dried dill
½ teaspoon cumin
1 tablespoon soy sauce

Place all of the ingredients in a large pot and bring to a boil. Reduce the heat to low. Cover and simmer for about 1 hour, or until the vegetables are soft.

VARIATIONS

1. Use red lentils and add chopped tomatoes or tomato paste.

2. Chopped chard is also a tasty addition.

Miso Soup

This soup does not store well, so make it fresh for each meal.

4 cups water
1 medium carrot, chopped
2 sliced mushrooms (shitake is the most flavorful kind and can be found dried in packs)
1 bunch green onions, chopped
1 pound silken tofu, cubed
1 cup broccoli florets
½–¾ cup golden miso paste

Place all of the ingredients except the miso paste in a large pot and bring to a boil. Reduce the heat to low, cover, and simmer for about 1 hour.

Stir in the miso paste and simmer for 15 minutes. Chicken or shrimp is also good in this soup.

Carrot Soup

5 tablespoons olive oil
2 onions, minced
3 garlic cloves, minced
4 cups minced carrots
1 cup minced yam
$\frac{1}{3}$ cup minced red bell pepper
2 tablespoons olive oil
6 cups vegetable stock
2 tablespoons soy sauce
1 tablespoon dill
Pinch of salt
Dash of pepper

Heat 3 tablespoons of the olive oil in a skillet over medium-high heat. Sauté the onions and garlic until the onions are translucent, about 8 minutes. Add the carrots, yam, red pepper, and the remaining 2 tablespoons olive oil and sauté for 5 minutes.

Add the stock, soy sauce, dill, salt, and pepper and bring to a boil. Reduce the heat to low and simmer for 20 minutes. Remove from the heat and allow to cool for 1 hour.

Puree the soup in batches in a blender.

Adding vegetables and white beans makes a great sauce to serve over couscous.

Kidney Bean Soup

2 cups cooked kidney beans
$1\frac{1}{2}$ quarts Vegetable Soup (see page 88)
2 cups chopped tomato
$\frac{1}{4}$ cup chopped cilantro
1 teaspoon finely chopped jalapeño pepper (optional)

Combine the kidney beans and vegetable soup in a large saucepan and simmer over low heat. Add the tomato, cilantro, and jalapeño pepper (if using). Cover and continue to simmer for 35 to 45 minutes.

Moroccan Vegetable Gumbo

$1\frac{1}{2}$ cup cooked red beans
3 onions, sliced

4 garlic cloves, minced
1 cup chopped celery
1½ cups diced carrot
3 cups diced sweet potatoes
1 cup diced zucchini
½ cup sliced red pepper
1½ cup chopped tomatoes
3 cups vegetable stock
1 cup tomato juice or sauce
1 tablespoon cumin
1 tablespoon coriander
1 tablespoon turmeric
½ teaspoon cinnamon
1 teaspoon soy sauce
2 tablespoons honey
Dash of cayenne pepper
Dash of paprika
Pinch of saffron
½ cup raisins

Combine all of the ingredients except the raisins in a large saucepan. Make sure the liquid reaches three-quarters of the way to the top of the vegetables. Cover and simmer over low heat for 45 minutes. Add the raisin and continue cooking for 10 more minutes. Add the beans. If you need more liquid, add more stock. Adjust the seasonings to your taste. Serve with warm rice.

Entrées

All of these recipes are vegan. In parentheses, I have included chicken, fish, or meat substitutions. If you decide to use chicken, fish, or meat, prepare it using the least fatty method, such as broiling or boiling. But try the vegan recipes first. You might be pleasantly surprised!

I realize that the dishes I offer in the thirty-day meal plan might seem a bit overwhelming to prepare at first. That is why I'm including these easy-to-make entrees. None should take more than thirty minutes to prepare. You can substitute by using your favorite vegetables, adding a chili pepper if you desire, garnishing with chopped peanuts, or serving on rice, soy pastas, or any grains you like. Have fun experimenting with these dishes.

Finally, make more than enough for one meal. These dishes all serve up well for lunch or a snack for the next day. They'll even keep for a few days sealed in a container in the refrigerator.

Butternut Squash Risotto

3 tablespoons olive oil
1 pound tofu, cubed (or chicken or shrimp)
½ teaspoon soy sauce (or tamari)
1 small butternut squash, cubed
1 cup green beans, cut into 1-inch pieces
3–4 cut leeks
6–8 sliced mushrooms
¼ cup powdered vegetable stock
2 cups plain soy milk
2 cups cooked short-grain brown rice

Heat 1 tablespoon of the olive oil in a skillet over medium-high heat. Sauté the tofu until browned and cooked through, about 5 minutes. Add the soy sauce and remove the tofu to a separate bowl.

Place the squash in a saucepan with just enough water to cover it and steam for about 12 minutes. (You can also steam the squash in a steamer.) Drain the squash and add it to the tofu.

Using the same saucepan, add the green beans with just enough water to cover them and steam for about 12 minutes. (You can also steam the beans in a steamer.) Drain the beans and add them to the bowl with the tofu and the squash.

Add the remaining 2 tablespoons olive oil to the skillet and sauté the leeks for 5 minutes. Add the mushrooms and sauté for another 5 minutes.

Add the tofu, squash, and green beans to the skillet. Sprinkle with the vegetable stock and mix to combine.

Stir in the soy milk and simmer for 10 minutes. Add the cooked rice. Spoon gently together and serve.

Broccoli and Tofu with Mushroom Sauce

8 large broccoli florets with 2-inch stems
2 cups oat flour
1 cup rice flour
1 cup cornmeal

2 tablespoons crushed flaxseeds
6 tablespoons water
1 pound extra-firm tofu

Mushroom Sauce
2 tablespoons canola oil
1 tablespoon butter
2 tablespoons minced garlic
3 bunches green onions
1½ pounds white mushrooms
½ cup chopped parsley
Juice of 1 lemon
6 cups vegetable stock
½ cup tamari
1 teaspoon dried thyme
1 cup dry sherry

Preheat the oven to 350 degrees F.

Place the broccoli in a saucepan with just enough water to cover and steam for about 8 minutes. (You can also steam the broccoli in a steamer.) Drain and set aside.

Mix the flours and cornmeal together in a large bowl. In a small bowl, mix the flaxseeds with the water.

Lay the tofu flat on a cutting board and slice it into ¼-inch-thick pieces the shape of a credit card. You should get 8 slices.

Spray a baking pan with oil spray. "Bread" the tofu by dredging each slice in the flour mix first, then in the flax mixture, and again in the flour mixture, coating it well. Place the slices on the baking sheet. Spray the tofu generously with oil and bake for 15 minutes.

To make the mushroom sauce: Heat the canola oil and butter in a skillet over medium-high heat. Sauté the garlic and onions until the onions are translucent, about 8 minutes. Add the mushrooms and keep stirring for 2 minutes. Add the parsley, lemon juice, vegetable stock, tamari, and thyme. Bring the mixture to a boil, then reduce the heat to low, cover, and simmer for 20 minutes.

Add the sherry to a small saucepan and bring to a boil. Twist the pot around a little until the sherry catches fire inside. Place the pot back on the burner and turn off the heat. When the flame in the pot goes out, the alcohol will be gone and only the flavor will remain. Add ½ cup of the reduced sherry to the sauce and discard the rest. Simmer for another 20 minutes.

To serve, pour half a cup of the sauce onto a plate and top with two pieces each of tofu and broccoli.

Tip: If the sauce is stored in the refrigerator overnight, the butter will rise to the top and can be scooped off easily. The sauce also freezes well.

Mushroom and Vegetable Risotto

1 pound extra-firm tofu, cut into ½-inch cubes
2 tablespoons toasted sesame oil
2 tablespoons canola oil
1 large onion, sliced thinly
3 garlic cloves, minced
2 medium carrots, julienned in 3-inch strips
4 stalks celery, julienned
1 medium-size zucchini, julienned
1½ cup sliced white mushrooms
½ cup sliced thinly green bell pepper
½ cup sliced thinly red bell pepper
4 cups cooked short-grain brown rice
2 cups vegetable stock
1 tablespoon tamari

Toss the tofu with the sesame oil in a medium bowl. Set aside.

Heat the canola oil in a skillet over medium-high heat. Sauté the onion and garlic until the onion is translucent, about 8 minutes. Add the carrots, celery, zucchini, mushrooms, green pepper, and red pepper. Continue to sauté for 5 minutes.

Add the cooked rice and the tofu to the saucepan. Stir to combine well. Next, add the stock and the tamari and keep stirring. Simmer until the liquid is almost gone. Remove from the heat and let sit for 10 minutes. Serve warm.

Mashed Potatoes with Cauliflower and Gravy

3 pounds white potatoes
1 tablespoon canola oil
½ cup chopped onion
1 cup cauliflower
2 tablespoons olive oil
1 cup soy milk
1 teaspoon granulated garlic

Pinch of salt
Dash of ground pepper

Brown Gravy
1 medium white potato (unpeeled), cut into ¼-inch cubes
1 sprig fresh dill
1 sprig fresh thyme
3 tablespoons of olive oil
1 cup chopped onion
3 garlic cloves, minced
3 cups diced mushrooms
3 cups vegetable stock
2 tablespoons tamari
Dash of ground pepper

To make the mashed potatoes and cauliflower: Peel the potatoes and cut into cubes. Place the potatoes into a large pot and add enough water to cover. Boil over medium-high heat until the potatoes are soft, about 20 minutes. Remove from the heat, drain, and set aside.

Heat the canola oil in a skillet over medium-high heat. Sauté the onion until it is translucent, about 8 minutes.

Place the cauliflower in a large pot with enough water to cover and bring to a boil. Reduce the heat to medium and cook the cauliflower until it is soft, about 8 minutes. Remove from the heat, drain, and set aside.

Add the potatoes, cauliflower, onions, olive oil, ½ cup of the soy milk, the garlic, salt, and pepper to the bowl of a food processor. Pulse on and off while adding the remaining ½ cup soy milk.

To make the brown gravy: Place the potato cubes, thyme, and dill in a medium pot with enough water to cover. Boil over medium-high heat until the potatoes are soft, about 20 minutes. Remove the thyme and dill and drain.

Heat the olive oil in a skillet over medium-high heat. Sauté the onion and garlic until the onion is translucent, about 8 minutes. Add the mushrooms and sauté for 5 minutes.

Bring the stock to a boil in a separate pot over medium-high heat. Reduce the heat to low and simmer for 15 to 20 minutes.

Place the potato cubes and the onion-mushroom mixture in a food processor. Pulse while slowly adding the stock ¼ cup at a time until combined. Add the tamari and pepper.

Vegetables with Tofu and Peanut Sauce

5 tablespoons olive oil
1 tablespoon sesame oil
1 pound extra-firm tofu, cut into ¼-inch cubes
5 tablespoons tamari
1 large onion, diced
3 garlic cloves, minced
3 tablespoons olive oil
1 cup chopped carrot
1 cup chopped celery
1 cup diced mixed peppers
1 cup shredded chard
1 cup shredded Napa cabbage
½ cup almond butter
½ cup chopped peanuts

Heat 2 tablespoons of the olive oil and the sesame oil in a skillet over medium-high heat. Sauté the tofu cubes until tender, turning to brown all sides, about 5 minutes. Add 1½ tablespoons of the tamari and turn the cubes quickly to cover all the pieces. Remove the tofu to a bowl to cool. In the same skillet, sauté the onion and garlic in the remaining 3 tablespoons olive oil until the onion is translucent, about 8 minutes. Add the carrots, celery, and peppers and cook for 5 minutes.

Add the chard and cabbage and toss. Add 2 tablespoons of tamari and mix well.

In a saucepan, cook the remaining 1½ tablespoons tamari and the almond butter over low heat. Stir until the sauce is well combined and smooth. Add the chopped peanuts and mix well. Stir the sauce into the vegetable mixture.

Serve over short-grain brown rice or rice pasta.

Tofu Lettuce Cups

1 pound firm tofu
½ cup soy sauce
½ cup water
3 tablespoons toasted sesame oil
1 tablespoon minced ginger
1 tablespoon minced garlic
1½ tablespoons sesame oil

½ bunch of cilantro, chopped
1 bunch of green onions, chopped
1 can sliced water chestnuts, chopped
1 tablespoon cornstarch
2 tablespoons cold water
10 large lettuce leaves

Slice the tofu into strips. Combine the soy sauce, water, toasted sesame oil, ginger, and garlic in large bowl. Add the tofu, cover, and marinate for 3 hours.

Drain the tofu and reserve the marinade. Dice the tofu. Heat the sesame oil in a skillet and sauté the tofu for 5 to 6 minutes.

Remove the tofu to a large bowl and combine with the cilantro, green onions, and water chestnuts.

In a saucepan, bring the marinade to a boil over medium-high heat.

Mix the cornstarch and water in a small bowl and slowly add to the hot marinade. Reduce the heat to medium and stir constantly for about 30 seconds so that the sauce thickens slightly. Add some of this liquid to the tofu and toss.

Wash and dry the lettuce leaves. Use the leaves as "pancakes" and fill each one with a large spoonful of the tofu mixture. Wrap up as for a crepe.

Broccoli and Cauliflower Sauté

8 cups water
1 bunch of broccoli, cut into pieces with 2-inch stems
2 cups cauliflower pieces, without stems
¾ cup chopped green onions
3 garlic cloves, minced
3 tablespoons toasted sesame oil
1 cup sliced mushrooms
1½ tablespoons soy sauce
½ cup sesame seeds

Bring the water to a boil and add the broccoli and cauliflower. Cook for 5 minutes, drain, and set aside.

Heat the sesame oil in a skillet over medium-high heat. Sauté the onions and garlic until the onion is translucent, about 8 minutes. Add the mushrooms, toss, and sauté for 3 minutes.

Add the broccoli and cauliflower and mix well. Add the soy sauce and mix well.

Put the sesame seeds in a small saucepan and heat for 3 to 5 minutes until brown, shaking the pan over the burner. Sprinkle the toasted sesame seeds over the vegetables.

Braised Tofu

1–2 pounds extra-firm tofu
2 tablespoons toasted sesame oil
2 tablespoons olive oil
1 tablespoon peanut oil
2 tablespoons minced garlic
3 tablespoons soy sauce
1 tablespoon powdered soup stock

Preheat the oven to 350 degrees F.
Cut the tofu into $\frac{1}{4}$-inch-thick triangles or $\frac{3}{8}$-inch strips and set aside.

Combine all of the other ingredients in a large bowl. Add the tofu and mix gently until all of the pieces are coated with oil.

Place the tofu on a baking tray and bake for 10 minutes. Turn over the tofu slices and bake for another 10 minutes. (You can also sauté the tofu in a skillet for about 5 minutes, turning to brown all sides.)

The remaining liquid can be poured on the tofu as it is baking or sautéing.

Vegetable Pilaf

4 tablespoons olive oil
1 cup chopped white onion
$\frac{1}{2}$ cup chopped green onions
3 garlic cloves, minced
2-inch piece of ginger, peeled and chopped
2 cups sliced mushrooms
1 cup chopped carrots
1 cup chopped celery
$\frac{1}{2}$ cup green bell peppers
$\frac{1}{2}$ cup fresh or defrosted frozen peas
$\frac{1}{2}$ cup corn kernels
$1\frac{1}{2}$ cups vegetable stock

2½ tablespoons soy sauce
4 cups cooked basmati rice

Heat 2 tablespoons of the olive oil in a skillet over medium-high heat. Sauté the onions, garlic, and ginger until the onion is translucent, about 8 minutes.

Add another tablespoon of oil and the sliced mushrooms. Toss and sauté for 5 minutes.

Add the remaining tablespoon oil and the carrots, celery, green pepper, peas, and corn to the skillet. Mix well and continue to cook for 2 minutes. Add the stock and soy sauce. Lower the heat, cover, and simmer for 8 minutes.

Serve over the basmati rice.

Green Vegetable Risotto

3 tablespoons olive oil
1 cup chopped green onions
4 garlic cloves, minced
2 cups sliced white mushrooms
3½ cups vegetable stock
1 cup small broccoli florets
⅓ cup chopped green bell pepper
5 asparagus stalks, cut into 1-inch pieces
½ cup peas
2 cups shredded bok choy or white cabbage
2 tablespoons tamari
1 cup cooked white beans or raw fava beans
3 cups cooked long-grain white rice
½ cup chopped parsley (optional)

Heat 2 tablespoons of the olive oil in a skillet over medium-high heat. Sauté the onion and the garlic until the onion is translucent, about 8 minutes. Add the remaining tablespoon oil and the mushrooms. Sauté for 3 minutes. Add 2 cups of the stock and the broccoli, green pepper, asparagus, peas, bok choy, tamari, and beans. Lower the heat, cover, and simmer for 10 minutes. Add more stock if needed.

Add the rice and the remaining stock. Continue to simmer until all the liquid is absorbed, about 10 minutes.

Garnish with the chopped parsley, if desired.

Winter Squash Stew

This recipe calls for hubbard and kabocha squashes, but you can choose any mix of winter squashes that make up 6 cups.

2 cups cubed hubbard squash
2 cups cubed kabocha squash
2 cups cubed sweet potatoes
1 cup chopped carrot
2 tablespoons olive oil
2 onions, cut into 1-inch chunks
4 garlic cloves, minced
3-inch piece of fresh ginger, peeled and minced
1 teaspoon dried marjoram
½ teaspoon cinnamon
1 tablespoon soy sauce
¼ teaspoon white pepper
2 cups vegetable stock
1½ cup cooked navy beans
3 cups cooked short-grain brown rice

Place the squashes, sweet potato, and carrots in a large pot and cover with water. Boil over medium-high heat until the vegetables are soft, about 15 minutes. Drain and set aside.

Heat the olive oil in a skillet over medium-high heat. Sauté the onions, garlic, and ginger until the onions are translucent, about 8 minutes. Add the squashes and carrot to the skillet and toss. Add the marjoram, cinnamon, soy sauce, and pepper and stir to combine. And the stock and navy beans. Reduce the heat to low, cover, and simmer for 10 minutes.

Serve over the brown rice.

Stuffed Wontons

You can buy wonton wrappers at your local Asian foods market, or check your regular supermarket as some carry the wrappers in their Asian foods sections. Read the labels carefully. Look for packaged wontons without additives.

1 teaspoon sesame oil
1 teaspoon soy oil
1- to 2-inch piece of ginger, sliced lengthwise

1 onion, chopped
2 carrots, grated
½ cup chopped celery
1 cup minced mushrooms
1 tablespoon soy sauce
½ cup oat or spelt bread crumbs
30 wonton wrappers

Heat the oils in a skillet or a wok over medium-high heat. Add the ginger, onion, carrots, and celery and stir-fry for 6 minutes. Add the mushrooms and continue stir-frying for another 2 minutes. Add the soy sauce. Turn off the heat and spoon the vegetables into a bowl. Add the bread crumbs and mix well. Set aside and allow to cool for 30 minutes.

To assemble the wontons: Have a small bowl of water handy. Lay out a wonton wrapper on a flat surface. Spoon 1 teaspoon of the filling into the center. Dip a clean finger into the water and wet two adjacent edges of the wonton wrapper. Fold the other two edges over to form a triangle shape and press them together. Place the finished wontons on a baking sheet.

Set up a steamer. Lightly oil the basket and steam the wontons for 2 minutes.

Serve the wontons with peanut sauce or soy sauce. The wontons can be made the day before and sealed with plastic wrap and stored in the refrigerator.

Stuffed Zucchini   Serves 4 (about 2 boats per person)

4 6-inch long zucchini
2 tablespoons olive oil
½ cup chopped green onions
½ cup chopped white onion
½ cup chopped celery
3 garlic cloves, minced
1½ cups sliced button mushrooms
1 tablespoon soy sauce
½ cup bread crumbs
½ teaspoon dried dill
Dash of cayenne
Paprika

Preheat the oven to 350 degrees F.

Wash the zucchini and slice in half lengthwise. Scoop out the pulp. Chop the pulp and reserve.

Heat the oil in a skillet over medium-high heat. Add the onions, celery, and garlic and sauté until the onions are translucent, about 8 minutes. Add the mushrooms, stir well, and sauté for another 3 minutes.

Add the zucchini pulp and combine well. Add the soy sauce and transfer the mixture to a bowl. Add the bread crumbs, dill, and cayenne.

Fill the sliced zucchini boats with the mushroom mixture and top with a dash of paprika.

Place the filled zucchini boats in a baking dish and bake for 25 minutes. Serve warm.

Tofu Lasagna   Serves 6–8

2 pounds firm tofu
1 tablespoon olive oil
3 white onions, chopped
4 garlic cloves, minced
3 cups grated carrots
3 cups chopped celery
4 cups sliced mushrooms
3 cups chopped zucchini
3 cups chopped broccoli
3 cups chopped green or red chard
5 cups tomato sauce (see the recipe for Pasta with Tomato Sauce on
    page 111)
3 cups grated soy mozzarella cheese

Preheat the oven to 375 degrees F.

Cut the tofu into $\frac{1}{8}$-inch-thick slices. Keep the length the size of the 1-pound block. Each piece should be about $4\frac{1}{2} \times 2\frac{1}{2} \times \frac{1}{8}$-inch thick. There should be about 20 pieces.

Heat the oil in a skillet over medium heat. Sauté the onions and garlic until the onions are translucent, about 8 minutes. Add the carrots, celery, and mushrooms and continue to sauté for another 5 minutes, stirring occasionally. Add the zucchini, broccoli, and chard and sauté for 5 more minutes. Transfer the vegetables to a bowl and set aside.

To assemble the lasagna: In a 12 × 16 × 3-inch casserole, spoon $\frac{3}{4}$ cup of the tomato sauce, covering the entire bottom of the casserole, and then lay out the slabs of tofu end to end. Pour half of the vegetable mix on top and carefully spread it out.

Sprinkle 1 cup of the soy cheese evenly on top. Then pour on 1½ cups of the tomato sauce and spread it evenly. Repeat, starting with the tofu, then top with the vegetable mix, and finish with a layer of tofu, soy cheese, and tomato sauce.

Cover the casserole dish and bake for 1½ hours. Remove the cover and bake for 20 minutes more.

Avocado and Rice Sushi   Makes 8 rolls

To make the sushi rolls, purchase a rolling mat from your local health food or Asian store.

2 cups cooked brown rice
¼ cup rice wine vinegar
2 tablespoons honey
1 tablespoon soy sauce or tamari
4 green onions, split lengthwise
8 strips of carrot, about 6 inches long
16 slices of avocado
16 strips of tofu, about 3 inches long, ¼ inch wide, and ¼ inch thick
8 rolls of nori seaweed

Combine the cooked rice in a bowl with the vinegar, honey, and soy sauce. Set aside. Have the vegetables and tofu ready on a platter.

Place a piece of nori seaweed on the rolling mat. With wet fingertips, pat a layer of rice about ⅛ inch thick onto the seaweed, covering the whole surface. Arrange small portions of the onions, carrot, avocado, and tofu in horizontal lines down the center of the seaweed. Take the edge of the mat and, using your fingers, roll up the whole thing tightly. Cut into 1-inch rolls and serve.

Barbecued Tofu

¾ cup water
2 tablespoons soy sauce
2 tablespoons red wine vinegar
1 teaspoon granulated garlic
1 pound firm tofu, cut into 3 × 1 × ¼-inch strips
½ cup tomato sauce (see the recipe for Pasta with Tomato Sauce on page 111)

2 tablespoons honey
1 tablespoon molasses
¼ cup chopped white onion
2 garlic cloves, minced
1 tablespoon vinegar
Dash of soy sauce
2 cups cooked short-grain brown rice

Set the oven to broil.

Combine ½ cup of the water, the soy sauce, red wine vinegar, and granulated garlic in a bowl. Marinate the tofu strips in this mixture for 30 minutes.

Combine the tomato sauce, remaining ¼ cup water, the honey, molasses, onion, garlic cloves, vinegar, and soy sauce in a saucepan. Simmer over low heat until the honey is dissolved, about 10 minutes.

Remove the tofu from the marinade. Line the tofu strips in a baking dish. Lightly broil the tofu strips in the oven, about 7 minutes. Remove the tofu from the oven and pour the sauce on top. Return the pan to the oven and broil for a few minutes until the tofu is browned.

Serve on a bed of brown rice.

Burritos with Refried Beans

2 tablespoon molasses
¼ cup honey
½ cup tomato sauce (see the recipe for Pasta with Tomato Sauce on
    page 111)
2 cups cooked pinto or black beans
2 cups cooked short-grain brown rice
Corn tortillas

In a saucepan, combine the molasses, honey, tomato sauce, and beans. Cook over medium-low heat, stirring constantly. If the beans begin to stick to the pan, scrape the bottom with a wooden spoon. When the beans are tender and the liquid has turned "saucy" (in 8 to 10 minutes), remove from the heat.

Layer the rice and the refried beans onto tortillas and roll up tightly to make a burrito. This can be done before the meal is served or the ingredients can be placed on the dinner table so everyone can make his or her own. This dish goes great with Salsa (see page 67).

Cuban-Chinese Rice and Beans

1 tablespoon olive oil
1 white onion, chopped
½ cup chopped green onions
2 garlic cloves, chopped
1 jalapeño pepper, chopped (if you like spicy food, do not remove the seeds;
    if you like mild tastes, remove the seeds)
¼ cup chopped cilantro
1 cup chopped tomato
¼ cup chopped black olives
¼ cup chopped green bell pepper
1 teaspoon cumin
1 teaspoon paprika
1 tablespoon soy sauce
2 cups mung bean sprouts
2 cups cooked black beans
3 cups cooked short-grain brown rice

Heat the olive oil in a skillet over medium-high heat. Sauté the onions, garlic, and jalapeño pepper over medium heat until the onions are translucent, about 8 minutes. Add the cilantro, tomato, olives, green pepper, cumin, paprika, soy sauce, and bean sprouts and combine well. Add the cooked black beans. Cook over medium-low heat until hot, about 10 minutes. Serve over the brown rice.

Greek Potatoes

3–4 lbs baking potatoes, cut into ½-inch cubes
1 teaspoon olive oil
1 cup lemon juice
2 garlic cloves, minced
2 teaspoons dried oregano
½ cup chopped green onions
1 teaspoon soy sauce
Dash of freshly ground black pepper
Chopped parsley (optional)

Place the potatoes in a large saucepan and cover with water. Boil over medium-high heat for 20 minutes until tender. Drain the potatoes and set aside.

Heat the olive oil in a skillet over medium-high heat. Sauté the lemon juice, garlic, oregano, and onion until the onion is translucent, about 8 minutes. Add the potatoes and cook, stirring so the potatoes don't stick to the sides. Add the soy sauce and pepper.

Serve hot, garnished with chopped parsley, if using.

Indian Pancakes (Dosas) with Masala Potatoes

Dosas
2 cups brown rice flour
½ cup soy flour
3 cups water
Dash of salt

Masala Potatoes
2 medium baking potatoes
1 tablespoon olive oil
1 teaspoon mustard seeds
½ teaspoon cumin
½ teaspoon coriander
1 tablespoon cilantro leaves
1 tablespoon turmeric
1 tablespoon soy sauce
½ cup chopped onion
1 cup vegetable broth

To make the dosas: Heat a griddle over medium heat.

Combine the brown rice flour, soy flour, water, and salt in a large bowl. Drop 3 tablespoons of batter onto the hot griddle for each dosa.

To make the masala potatoes: Preheat the oven to 400 degrees F. Bake the potatoes for 45 to 60 minutes, remove from the oven, and allow to cool. When the potatoes have cooled, cut them into 1-inch pieces.

Heat the oil in a skillet over medium heat. Add the mustard seeds. When the seeds begin to pop, add the cumin, coriander, cilantro, turmeric, and soy sauce. Combine well and add the onion. Sauté for 5 minutes and then add the cooled pieces of potato. Add the broth and simmer uncovered for 15 minutes over low heat, combining all the ingredients well.

Serve with Dal (see page 66).

Korean Vegetable Pancakes with Soy Dipping Sauce
Serves 3–4

Although they're called "pancakes" here, these are typically eaten for lunch or as a dinner entrée. This dish is sometimes made with chopped seafood (squid, shrimp, and scallops) added to the batter, but this vegetarian variation is just as tasty.

Pancakes
1 cup cold water
1 cup gluten-free flour
½ cup rice flour
1 tablespoon crushed flaxseeds, mixed into 3 tablespoons water
1 teaspoon soy sauce or tamari
Pinch of salt
1 teaspoon honey
½ teaspoon miso paste
6 green onions, chopped
½ white onion, sliced thinly
½ carrot, julienned
2 tablespoons olive oil

Dipping Sauce
½ cup soy sauce
½ rice vinegar
½ green onion, chopped
½ jalapeño pepper, chopped
Pinch of red pepper flakes

To make the pancakes: In a large bowl, combine the water, flours, flaxseed mixture, soy sauce, salt, honey, and miso paste into a batter. (The colder the water, the crispier the pancakes will be.) When the batter is smooth, add the onions and carrot.

Heat the oil in a skillet over medium heat. Drop spoonfuls of batter into the pan to make pancakes that are 4 to 5 inches in diameter, and cook until brown, 2 to 3 minutes. Flip to the other side and brown for another 2 to 3 minutes.

To make the dipping sauce: Mix all of the ingredients in a small bowl. The amounts given above are just suggestions; adjust them to your tastes.

Pasta with Tomato Sauce

2 carrots, chopped
4 stalks of celery, chopped
1 onion, sliced
4 pounds Italian plum tomatoes, chopped
1 large can tomato paste
½ cup water
1 tablespoon dried basil leaves
1 bay leaf
½ tablespoon dried oregano
1 teaspoon granulated garlic

Place the carrots, celery, and onion in a large pot and cover with water. Bring to a boil over medium heat. Lower the heat and simmer for 15 minutes, uncovered. Remove the pot from the heat and allow the vegetables to cool slightly. Drain the vegetables, reserving the liquid. Add the vegetables and some of the liquid to a blender and blend to make a puree.

To make the tomato sauce: Add the tomatoes, tomato paste, water, basil, bay leaf, oregano, and garlic to a large stockpot. Simmer uncovered for 1 hour over low heat. Stir occasionally so the sauce doesn't stick to the pot. When the sauce is done, add the vegetable puree mixture.

Serve over rice or soy pasta.

"Pork" and Beans

In health food stores, and now in many supermarkets, you can find an assortment of soy "hot dogs." Pick your family's favorite for this dish.

1 package soy frankfurters
3 cups cooked red kidney beans
1 onion, chopped
1 garlic clove, minced
1 tomato, chopped

Split the franks lengthwise and place them on the grill or the griddle to cook. Heat until they are cooked through, about 10 minutes. Set aside.

Add the cooked beans, the onion, garlic, and tomato to a skillet. Sauté over low heat, scraping the bottom of the pan so the beans don't stick, for about 8 minutes.

Cut the franks into 1-inch pieces and add to the bean mixture. Heat through, about 5 minutes.

Serve hot.

Shish Kebab with Tofu on Basmati Rice

2 tablespoons soy sauce
¼ cup dry sherry
4 garlic cloves, pressed or minced
3 green onions, minced
¼ cup peanut sauce or honey
½ cup water
2 cups extra-firm tofu, cut into 1-inch cubes (or large enough to skewer)
1 red bell pepper, cut into wide strips
1 green bell pepper, cut into wide strips
2 carrots, cut into rounds ¼ inch thick
1 cup pearl onions
1 pound button mushrooms
1½ cup cherry tomatoes
1 cup cooked basmati rice

Stir together the soy sauce, sherry, garlic, green onions, peanut sauce, and water in a large bowl. When combined well, gently toss in the tofu and let it sit in the marinade for 1 hour.

Remove the tofu from the marinade with a slotted spoon and place in a bowl. Toss the peppers, carrots, pearl onions, mushrooms, and tomatoes gently in the marinade.

Take skewers or sticks and spear the vegetables and tofu in a colorful order. Place all the spears in a baking dish and pour the marinade over them. Turn the skewers several times to wet all of the vegetables.

Barbecue, grill, or broil the skewers in the oven until the vegetables and tofu are brown and cooked through.

Serve over basmati rice, with a soy dipping sauce if desired (see the recipe for Korean Vegetable Pancakes with Soy Dipping Sauce on page 110).

Corn and Bean Nachos

2 large bags of no-oil, baked corn tortilla chips
3 cups refried beans
2 cups cooked corn kernels

½ cup shredded carrots
1½ cup grated soy cheese
2 cups Guacamole (see page 64, or store-bought)
1 cup Salsa (see page 67, or store-bought)

Preheat the oven to 350 degrees F.

Line a baking dish with half of the tortilla chips. Layer the refried beans on top and then the corn kernels. Spread out the carrots and sprinkle with the soy cheese.

Surround the nachos with the remaining chips and bake for 20 minutes. Remove the dish from the oven and garnish with the guacamole and salsa.

Soy Cheese Pizza

You can buy pizza dough or pizza pie shells, soy or not, but here's a recipe you can make from scratch. You can add your own vegetable tomato sauce (see the recipe for Pasta with Tomato Sauce on page 111) and the kids' favorite vegetables and top with grated soy cheese. Bake until the cheese is browned.

Pizza Dough
1 package dry yeast
1⅓ cups warm (not hot) water
Pinch of sugar
2 tablespoons olive oil
Dash of salt
3 cups sifted multigrain or soy flour

Combine the yeast, water, and sugar in a medium bowl. Cover and let stand in a warm place (the inside of an unlit gas oven is usually 85 degrees).

When the yeast rises, add the oil, salt, and yeast mix to the flour. Knead for about 10 minutes, and let rise once, covered, in a warm place for about 2 hours.

Preheat the oven to 400 degrees F.

Lightly oil two pizza pie pans (12-inch diameter) or a baking sheet. When the dough is ready, put it down on the pans and stretch it out to fill. Pinch up the edges to form a little wall to hold the sauce and vegetables. Prick the dough with a fork several times.

Spread tomato sauce and vegetables on the dough and top with grated soy cheese. Bake for about 30 minutes or until the cheese starts to brown.

Stir-Fry Vegetables with Brown Rice

2 cups short-grain brown rice
4½ cups cold water
2 tablespoons olive oil
2 medium onions, chopped
2 garlic cloves, chopped
1-inch piece of ginger, sliced lengthwise
3 carrots, cut into diagonal slices ⅛ inch thick
2 cups chopped celery
1 cup sliced mushrooms
1 small green bell pepper, sliced
1 small red bell pepper, sliced
1½ cups sliced zucchini or yellow squash
1 cup broccoli florets
1–2 tablespoons soy sauce or tamari
2 tablespoons toasted sesame seeds

Combine the rice and water in a saucepan and bring to a boil over high heat. Reduce the heat, cover, and simmer for 35 minutes. Turn off the heat. Leave the lid on and allow the rice to stand for 20 minutes.

Heat the oil in a skillet over medium-high heat. Add the onions, garlic, and ginger and sauté until the onions are translucent, about 8 minutes. Add the carrots, celery, mushrooms, peppers, zucchini, broccoli, and soy sauce and stir all the vegetables to coat. Continue to sauté for 2 to 3 minutes.

Serve hot over a bed of short-grain brown rice and top with the sesame seeds.

Stir-Fry with Tofu

1 tablespoon sesame oil
1 tablespoon soy oil
2 white onions, chopped
2 carrots, julienned
2-inch piece of ginger, cut lengthwise
3 garlic cloves, minced

½ cup chopped green onions
1 cup sliced shitake mushrooms
2 ounces prepared black mushrooms
1½ cups diced firm tofu
1 can water chestnuts, sliced
1 head of bok choy, washed well and sliced
2 cups mung bean sprouts
1–2 tablespoons soy sauce
¼ cup dry sherry or rice wine

Heat the oils in a skillet over medium-high heat. Add the white onions, carrots, ginger, garlic, and green onions and sauté until the onions are translucent, about 8 minutes. Then add the mushrooms, tofu, water chestnuts, and bok choy and sauté for another 5 minutes. Add the mung bean sprouts, soy sauce, and sherry. Reduce the heat to low and simmer uncovered for 3 minutes more.

Serve hot over a bed of short-grain brown rice.

Sweet-and-Sour Chinese Vegetables

1½ cups mushroom stock
1 tablespoon sesame oil
1 tablespoon canola oil
2 cups sliced white onions
½ cup chopped green onions
3 garlic cloves, minced
1-inch piece of ginger, sliced lengthwise in half
1 cup sliced small button mushrooms
2 cups carrots, sliced diagonally in ¼-inch-thick pieces
1½ cups celery, cut into 1-inch pieces
1 cup cauliflower florets
1 cup snow peas
2 cups shredded Chinese cabbage
1 cup sliced tomato
2 cups bottled sweet-and-sour sauce
½ cup chopped cashews or peanuts (optional)

To make the mushroom stock: Fill a large pot ¾ to the top with button mushrooms, cover with water, and boil. Reduce the heat and simmer for 1½ hours uncovered. Strain the mushrooms and leave the liquid stock. This can be done a few days in advance.

In a skillet or a wok, heat the oils over medium-high heat. Sauté the onions, garlic, and ginger, stirring occasionally, until the onions are translucent, about 8 minutes. Add the mushrooms and sauté for 3 minutes. Add the carrots, celery, cauliflower, snow peas, cabbage, and tomatoes, one vegetable at a time. Stir well after each addition. Add the stock. Mix well. Add the sweet-and-sour sauce. Reduce the heat to low, cover, and simmer, stirring occasionally, for about 20 minutes.

Serve over rice garnished with chopped nuts, if desired.

Desserts

Frozen Juice/Fruit Puree on a Stick

You can purchase molds at the grocery store to make this treat, which is similar to a Popsicle. Fill the mold with a mixture of ½ fruit juice/puree and ½ water. For variety, add diced fresh fruit, such as berries, peaches, or pineapple.

Fruit smoothies can also be poured into the molds and served frozen.

Baked Orange Slices

½ cup orange juice
½ cup apple juice
2 tablespoons honey
¼ cup raisins
Dash of cinnamon
Dash of nutmeg
2 or 3 oranges

Set the oven to broil.

Mix the orange juice, apple juice, honey, raisins, cinnamon, and nutmeg in a saucepan. Simmer uncovered over low heat until the honey is melted, about 3 minutes. Remove from the heat and set aside. Peel the oranges and slice them into quarters. Place the orange slices in a small baking dish and pour the sauce over them.

Broil the orange slices for 6 to 8 minutes, watching closely to prevent burning. The sauce should thicken slightly.

Serve hot.

Fruit Cobbler

6 slices peaches or pears (unpeeled)
½ cup multigrain flour
1 teaspoon cinnamon
Dash of nutmeg
½ cup orange juice
⅓ cup honey
2 tablespoons arrowroot dissolved in ¼ cup cold water
Chopped nuts or fat-free granola (optional)

Preheat the oven to 350 degrees F.

Combine the fruit, flour, cinnamon, and nutmeg in a large bowl and toss together. Pour the fruit mixture into a baking dish. In a saucepan, combine the orange juice, honey, and arrowroot mixture and heat over low heat until the honey is dissolved.

Pour the sauce over the fruit. Bake uncovered for 35 minutes.

Top with chopped nuts or fat-free granola, if desired. Serve warm.

Fruity Couscous Cake

5 cups apple juice
3 tablespoons lemon juice
1 tablespoon grated lemon zest
2 cups couscous
2 cups mixed fruit or berries (optional)
Toasted nuts (optional)

Combine the apple juice and lemon juice in a saucepan and bring to a boil over medium-high heat. Slowly add the lemon zest and couscous and stir until thick. Pour the mixture into a cake pan and combine with the fresh fruit. Allow to cool and then cover and chill in the refrigerator for 2 hours.

Cut into slices and top with fruit puree and toasted nuts, if desired.

Baked Apples with Strawberries

4 Granny Smith or Macintosh apples (preferably organic)
1 cup water
2 tablespoon honey

½ teaspoon cinnamon
Sprinkle of ground cloves

Preheat the oven to 350 degrees F.

Core the apples and place them standing up in a baking dish.

In a saucepan, combine the remaining ingredients. Heat the mixture over medium heat for 2 to 3 minutes. Pour the mixture over the apples. Bake uncovered for 35 minutes.

Remove the apples from oven and allow them to cool slightly. Serve with sliced strawberries and some of the cooking liquid poured over the apples. Top with chopped nuts.

Bananas in Fruit Sauce

1 cup fresh strawberries or ½ cup raspberries
1 tablespoon soy milk
½ teaspoon vanilla
2 bananas, sliced
Mint leaf (optional)

Place the berries, soy milk, and vanilla to a blender and blend until well combined. Arrange the banana slices in a circle and pour the puree over them. Top with a mint leaf, if desired.

Strawberry Tofu Cream

½ pound firm tofu
2 tablespoons honey
1 cup sliced strawberries
2 tablespoons maple syrup
1 tablespoon lemon juice
Dash of vanilla
Dash of nutmeg
Dash of cinnamon

Place all of the ingredients in a food processor and pulse until smooth. You may need to add a little water to achieve a creamy consistency. The tofu cream will keep for a few days in the refrigerator. If it separates, just whip it up again before serving.

Any fruit can be added in place of, or in addition to, the strawberries.

Tofu Banana Parfait   Serves 4

4 ounces silken tofu
1 small ripe banana, sliced
⅓ cup apple juice
3 tablespoons fruit puree
½ cup berries
1 large very ripe peach or papaya, peeled and diced
1 kiwi, peeled and sliced into thin rounds
4 mint leaves

Place the tofu, banana, apple juice, and fruit puree in a blender and blend until smooth. Freeze the mixture in an ice cube tray for 30 minutes, and then return to the blender. Blend until light and creamy.

In parfait glasses, place 1 tablespoon of berries and then some peach slices. Arrange 2 kiwi slices along the outside of the glass. Pour the tofu puree halfway up the glass. Finish adding the berries and peaches and top with the tofu puree. Top with a kiwi slice and a mint leaf. You can change the fruits according to seasonal availability.

Vanilla Almond Custard

½ pound silken tofu
6 tablespoons honey
1 tablespoon vanilla
3 drops almond extract
3 cups water
Juice from half a lemon
2 tablespoons soy milk
4 tablespoons agar-agar flakes
1 cup water

Place the tofu, honey, vanilla, almond extract, water, and lemon juice in a blender and blend until smooth. Slowly add the soy milk.

Combine the agar-agar and water in a small bowl. Stir until the agar-agar is dissolved. Pour the agar liquid into the custard.

Pour the mixture into molds, dessert cups, or a large bowl. Chill in the refrigerator uncovered until you are ready to serve.

VARIATIONS

1. Chocolate (Carob) Custard: eliminate the almond extract and substitute ¼ cup carob powder. Add 2 more tablespoons of honey if needed.

2. Strawberry Custard: eliminate the almond extract and add 1 cup strawberry puree. Top with fresh berries.

3. Banana Custard: eliminate the almond extract and add 1½ cups fresh banana slices and a dash of vanilla. Top with shredded coconut.

4. Orange Custard: eliminate the almond extract and 1 cup water and add 1 cup orange juice. Fresh orange slices or mandarin oranges make a great topping.

Tofu Cheesecake

Piecrust
1 cup oat flour
1 cup rolled oats
¼ teaspoon sea salt
⅓ cup olive oil
2–3 teaspoons water
2 cups dried beans

Filling
1 pound firm tofu
1 tablespoon peanut oil
¼ cup soy milk
1 teaspoon vanilla
½ cup lemon juice
2 tablespoons maple syrup
Dash of salt

To make the piecrust: Preheat the oven to 350 degrees.

Combine the flour, oats, and salt in a large bowl. Add the olive oil and mix into the dry ingredients with a fork. Add the water and continue mixing with a fork for 3 minutes. Let the dough stand for 5 minutes and then press into a pie plate. Prick the crust in several places with a fork.

Place a piece of parchment paper in the pie shell and fill with the beans. (The beans will weigh down the crust so it doesn't bubble.) Bake uncovered for 12 minutes. Remove from the oven and scoop out the beans and save for the next piecrust. You will not be able to use the beans for anything else.

To make the filling: Place all of the ingredients in a food processor and pulse until smooth. Pour into the prepared piecrust and bake uncovered for 45 minutes.

Tofu Pumpkin Pie

1 pound firm tofu
⅓ cup brown rice syrup
1 tablespoon barley malt syrup
1 tablespoon maple syrup
1(16-ounce) can pumpkin puree (without additives)
1 teaspoon cinnamon
Dash of allspice
Dash of nutmeg
1 piecrust (see the Tofu Cheesecake recipe on page 120)

Preheat the oven to 350 degrees F.

Place all of the ingredients in a food processor and pulse until smooth. Pour into the prepared piecrust and bake uncovered for 45 minutes.

Granola Bars

2½ cups rolled oats
¼ cup sesame seeds
¼ cup chopped pecans
¼ cup sunflower seeds
½ cup chopped cashews
¼ cup chopped figs or dates
½ cup almond butter
½ cup maple syrup

Preheat the oven to 325 degrees F.

Spray an 8 × 8-inch baking dish with oil.

Mix all of the ingredients together in a large bowl. Press into the baking dish. Bake uncovered for about 30 minutes.

Let cool in the baking dish for about 1 hour before cutting into bars. These bars store very well in a tightly covered container for a few days.

Variations:

1. Add ½ cup shredded coconut.
2. Add ½ cup dried fruit.
3. Add ¼ cup raisins.
4. Add ½ cup chopped apples.

PART II

The Details

4

No One Knows Your Child Better Than You Do

Living with a child who has ADD/ADHD or something like it can be hard, as you know. The media keep bringing this disorder to our attention. Parents now know that their children might not be intentionally difficult or oppositional; they need help in dealing with attention deficit disorder. Sometimes the ADD/ADHD label is applied in preschool, when a parent or a teacher notices that a child is harder to manage than the other children.

The classic signs that lead to an ADD/ADHD diagnosis are physically disruptive behavior and a lack of impulse control. Attention deficit may be very obvious in some children but more subtle in others. A "mild" ADD and impulse-control problem can still be very disruptive and distressing to parents and teachers. The diagnosis may not be made for quite a while because as long as these kids are surrounded by protective, accommodating family members, caregivers, and teachers and placed in small, informal preschool classrooms or other small-group social settings, they can manage reasonably well. Sure, they may move around when they should be still, talk out of turn, and have trouble with group activities because they don't pay attention or follow directions, but somehow their behavior never quite sabotages the group or the family.

The truth is, not all children with ADD/ADHD exhibit disruptive behavior (and not all children who exhibit these behaviors have ADD/ADHD). The symptoms of the disorder vary and can also include restlessness, irritability, lack of focus, difficulty following instructions, insomnia, and impulsive behavior or lack of self-control. As frustrating as these symptoms can be, there are ways to deal with them, lessen them, and even get rid of them.

The media often refer to ADD/ADHD as an epidemic, and this really isn't a stretch of the truth. The typical American diet, filled with sugar and processed food, doesn't allow healthy, optimal brain function.

Estimates vary widely, but several million school-age children have received an official diagnosis of ADD and ADHD, and twice as many display some of the symptoms of the disorders. According to the U.S. Centers for Disease Control and Prevention, roughly 8 percent of children between the ages of four and seventeen have ADD/ADHD, and more than 3 million of them are taking prescription medications to treat their symptoms.

What this means is that there are no classrooms, from preschool through high school, without two, three, four, or more students diagnosed with ADD/ADHD. Younger boys are three to four times more likely to be labeled with the disorder than girls (which appears to balance out around the fifth or six grade). As many as half of those who are diagnosed with ADD/ADHD when they are children continue to be affected by its symptoms as they become adults.

In my years in practice as a pediatrician, I have seen so many of these kids, and their families, struggle with this and the stigma that accompanies any mental-health condition. I've also treated lots of families and seen them grapple with this diagnosis and then struggle even more with the child's various treatment options. They are continually influenced by commercials and advertisements on television, the radio, or in magazines that tell them that medication is the easy and necessary solution to their children's behavioral problems. Then they are further confused when the media shift their focus to talking about the dangers of *over*-medicating children. These mixed messages have made for many difficult office consultations. My conclusion is while some children may eventually need pharmaceutical help, medication is definitely not the best first choice. The child and the parents need to be participants in the child's treatment, and I have to help them fully understand what is really going on and explain their nondrug options.

You know already that ADD/ADHD is very commonly treated with medication. Because it is difficult to raise and educate a son or a daughter with ADD/ADHD, families are often relieved to find out that medication may offer a quick fix. But I want parents to know that these medications are not "free": they cost the mind and the body a lot more than the cost of a prescription. The several million American children who spend their childhood and adolescence taking prescription stimulants risk a host of damaging side effects and potential long-term health issues, and they may even be setting the stage for ongoing drug misuse and abuse. Let's try to spare our children all this. With diligence and patience, a natural treatment program works. Again, even if medication is needed, the nutritional changes, exercise, improved sleep habits, and limit-setting described in this book will make the dose of medication smaller and the side effects minimal.

The diagnosis of ADD/ADHD puts the entire family through long periods and great amounts of unneeded stress, and the failure of treatments based on prescription drugs affects not only the child, who thinks he or she has failed, but also parents, caregivers, and siblings. From bouts of uncontrollable behavior to school suspensions to the stigmatizing of brothers and sisters because of their unruly sibling, the damage escalates quickly. Parents argue, children fight, and family vacations become impossible.

With so many families suffering, it is no wonder that the pharmaceutical industry has made an enormous effort to market drugs for ADD/ADHD. Our children's medical/social/academic ill fortune has become a billion-dollar business, and we're discovering that no miracle drug exists for this disorder. Medications that are pushed upon us as being solutions have significant side effects and really only treat the symptoms, not the condition.

I have found medication to be problematic. Unfortunately, we doctors are conditioned to automatically prescribe a set of drugs to match a diagnosis, and for ADD/ADHD, it's a prescription for mood-altering drugs. Many parents will also automatically accept all forms of treatment recommended by specialists and dismiss their own apprehensions in favor of trusting that the specialists know what is best for their children. Doctors must stop recommending these medications, and parents must start taking a more active role in their child's treatment, instead of merely administering the proper pills at the proper times.

Some families struggle with ADD/ADHD and with medications for years and years and see no way out. That isn't right. There should be a way out . . . and there is.

Doctors and other professionals can help, but only you can best decide what is best for your child. *No one knows your child better than you do.* If a school administrator or a doctor tells you that your child

---

What about Mom and Dad? The Whole Family May Have ADD/ADHD

We live in an ADD/ADHD world. We have personal digital assistants for instant e-mail, TiVos to watch television shows on demand, and cell phones to contact anybody anywhere at any time. All of these devices, and more, make life faster and faster and faster. When a family comes to see me for a consultation, the parents often smile in recognition as we discuss the symptoms of ADD/ADHD. That's because they've either been dealing with the symptoms themselves or their spouse has, and they didn't know it was a problem. Many of them didn't grow up in a time when ADD/ADHD was suggested or diagnosed.

Think about the following signs of the presence of ADD/ADHD, and consider whether they apply to you.

- Academic and/or Employment Problems
  - People with ADD/ADHD are more likely to have had to repeat a grade while they were in school.
  - They may underperform academically and in the workplace.
  - If you ask about job histories, you will often find that their pasts are full of job changes.
  - They may be unemployed and looking for work.
  - The may be underachieving in the workplace.
- Driving Problems
  - People with ADD/ADHD do more false braking than people in the population at large. They also are cited for more speeding tickets and moving violations.
  - People with ADD/ADHD are more likely to get into motor vehicle accidents. The accidents are also likely to be more severe.

needs to be evaluated for ADD/ADHD, listen closely but don't simply accept a diagnosis and the medication that goes with it. As you go through the evaluation, the diagnosis, and the treatment options, ask yourself often, "Are my child's symptoms posing any real danger to other children or caretakers? Are my child's symptoms really so bad that there's no hope of normal learning in school and making friends? Are my child's symptoms really so bad that we can't, as a family, deal with them without drugs?"

Follow your instincts when it comes to the decision to medicate your child immediately or to attempt a more natural, healthier lifestyle first.

- Negative Lifestyle Choices
  - People with ADD/ADHD are twice as likely to smoke as people who do not have the condition and are more inclined to drink beverages with caffeine.
  - People with ADD/ADHD are at an increased risk of developing substance-abuse disorders if not treated.
  - People with ADD/ADHD may have problems maintaining relationships.
  - An individual with ADD/ADHD is more likely to experience marital stress than a person without it.
  - Higher rates of divorce and separation exist for the population of people with ADD/ADHD than for the public at large.

If you've now begun to suspect that you might have more in common with your child than you previously thought, you should think about the diet on which *you* were raised. If you were fed plenty of junk foods and dairy while growing up (as many of us were, since we knew far less about health and diet back then), chances are you've been feeding your children the same kinds of things without a second thought. If your parents made you study longer hours than they allowed you to go outside to play and exercise, chances are you're raising your children with the same priorities.

This is precisely why no one knows your child better than you do and why dietary and lifestyle changes have to be family-wide. The ADD/ADHD cure may not only be saving your child a lifetime of frustration but it may also improve your life and your health in ways you never knew possible.

Your school administrators may not agree and your doctor may be skeptical, but do not lose sight of the fact that none of these people knows your child as well as you do, and none of them will have to deal with the negative side effects of the medication as much as your family will. Accept their help and their advice, but make sure they know that you will participate in all decisions when it comes to your child's health.

If eating healthy foods, getting your child to sleep more, and enforcing exercise do not significantly improve your child's behavioral problems, only *then* should you look into medication as a treatment option. I readily admit that I've seen families in crisis, where there was an urgent need for fast changes in behavior that only medication can bring. But the vast majority of families who are faced with these symptoms and/or a diagnosis of ADD/ADHD have time to explore natural remedies first.

Try the ADD/ADHD cure first. Take charge of your child's health. Let's do it together.

5

Taking Charge of Your Child's Health

The second you became a parent, your instincts kicked in and made you more suited to the role of caring for someone else. A diagnosis of ADD/ADHD can put a parent into red-alert mode. You find yourself wondering if your child is going to have this problem forever, whether he or she will be socially impaired, academically challenged, and unsuccessful in later life. You may actually become frightened that you're somehow not going to be able to protect your child or provide enough help for your child.

ADD/ADHD is trickier than most illnesses. You can spend hours explaining how your child behaves at home to a doctor, and he or she still might not truly understand the magnitude of the problem. Therefore your pediatrician might not be able to make recommendations about how you and your family can cope with your child's behavior problems without drugs. Most doctors are probably listening for key words and phrases—"trouble paying attention," "impulsive," or "hyperactive," for example—to help make a formal diagnosis; then they're more likely to "go by the book" and prescribe the pills designated for the disorder.

Your doctor may know your child well, but talking to you for thirty to forty minutes and then labeling your child as having ADD/ADHD isn't great medicine. The truth is, no one else is going to take full responsibility for your child. Taking charge of your child's health is the most important part of the ADD/ADHD cure. Take charge, with the goal of having full, drug-free control over your child's condition.

Trust your own instincts and your own parenting abilities, and then do the following:

- Assemble your support team
- Communicate with your child
- Educate your family and friends
- Inform your child's caregivers or school
- Set up successful interactions with other children
- Address the special needs of siblings

Assemble Your Support Team

Treating ADD/ADHD shouldn't be a private struggle. Most emotional illnesses have lost their social stigma, and while ADD/ADHD may be difficult to control, you can relax and share your problems with others. Your first task is to assemble your support team.

Parents, siblings, and extended family are affected, and everyone must work together to help your child. These commitments include family-wide changes to diet, exercise, and entertainment. Entertainment must not include video games. This must be enforced for all the children in your family, not just the one who has ADD/ADHD. It simply won't work or seem fair otherwise.

Sharing with other people will be an inspirational experience for you, as you realize just how much love and support your family really has. You'll find that while you've felt that your family has struggled privately and alone through your child's ADD/ADHD, there are many around you who are willing to help and to accommodate.

Family

Your family members all need to know that there will be changes to the kinds of food that everyone is used to eating. There will be less processed and sugar-laced food and less junk food in favor of fruits, vegetables, and healthy snacks. Everyone will exercise more. Tell your children that instead of watching TV and playing video games, the entire family will become more active by hiking, running, playing more, and engaging in other activities. Exercise alters the brain's chemistry, and family exercise can be the most fun of all. With these positive lifestyle changes, everybody wins by becoming healthier, and the child with ADD/ADHD wins most of all.

Siblings of children with ADD/ADHD (and, by the way, they might have ADD/ADHD themselves) might not get as much attention as they want or need from Mom or Dad. Often they witness their sibling being punished or yelled at, and they hear themselves being praised for their own contrasting behavior; they could begin to see themselves as the "good" kid. Conversely, the child with ADD/ADHD becomes the "bad" kid, and this can lead to the siblings' wanting nothing to do with the "problem child." Sit down with your other children and explain to them that their sibling has ADD/ADHD and needs special attention but that you will do all you can to make sure that they never feel unloved or unappreciated. This will help keep a potentially difficult situation from escalating out of control.

All in the Family: Factors That Inhibit ADD/ADHD Reversal

One of the cruelest ironies is that ADD/ADHD propels the family into crisis mode, so that members are constantly focusing on the urgent, not the important. These are the factors that inhibit the reversal of ADD/ADHD:

- ADD/ADHD disrupts your child's life, often isolating him or her from friends and siblings, which creates an emotional burden for the parents as well as the child.

- ADD/ADHD creates problems with your child's school, teachers, and caregivers, and the burden of resolution is often placed on the parents alone.

- ADD/ADHD is often genetic, leaving the parents to feel guilty for passing on a "bad gene" to their child.

- ADD/ADHD affects siblings, who are conflicted between their compassion for their brother or sister and wanting to separate themselves from the situation.

- ADD/ADHD causes undue stress and concern for the parents, who may not have the time and resources to address their own issues—including the inevitable relationship challenges.

Getting your other children active in the support team begins with a family discussion. Let your other children voice their frustrations, and you can explain yours as well. This is a great way to deepen the bond between you and your children. There are two things to keep in mind during this family discussion: do not place blame on anyone, and do not show anger.

For instance, instead of saying, "When he breaks things, it makes me so angry!" try saying, "I just don't know how to stop him from breaking things, and I should. Can we think of a way to help him together?" This is important so that the child you are speaking with does not identify their brother or sister as "the enemy" or someone who is hurting Mommy or Daddy. Instead, they'll see their brother or sister for who they really are: someone who needs love and care and a little extra help and attention.

For single-child families, the family support team consists of you and your spouse, or perhaps just you alone. If both parents are involved, the most important thing to do is clear the air as best you can. Don't leave unspoken any negative feelings you may have about your spouse not handling his or her share of the caregiving. You may find that he or she has the same complaint about you. Reexamine and outline your roles so that you can begin with a clean slate. Remember, the goal is not to place blame but to resolve all issues and open the lines of communication.

The mother and the father must be a team united with a strong desire to defend and help their child.

Friends and Relatives

We all know not to sneak peanuts to a child who is allergic to them. The same holds true for giving candy to a child with ADD/ADHD. Let your friends and relatives know that you will be avoiding certain trigger foods that can worsen symptoms and lead to behavioral issues. These friends and relatives will be your allies, whom you can trust to have your child's best interests in mind when you are not immediately available. In order for them to become proper allies, however, they must first be informed of and agree to the relationship.

Obviously, not everyone is going to have a sugar-free, dairy-free, and gluten-free birthday party, but your friends and family can help you instead of fighting you as you take care of your child's health needs. You'll be surprised at how many people will be supportive and accommodating if you just talk to them about the situation. For parents and family gatherings, call ahead or write a little note on the RSVP, just as you would if your child had allergies, diabetes, or any other condition that mandates a little extra attention and understanding.

Let anyone who can help know that you are taking a new approach to caring for your child and that you may need their assistance in the project. Arrange a supervised playdate. If any moms or dads have reservations, you can always assure them that you will be around to supervise and that a playdate will be useful to your child. Unfortunately, you will run across friends, relatives, and others who are not willing to cooperate and are endangering your child's health. You should limit the amount of contact you have with people who only know how to celebrate and have fun with sugar, French fries, and video games, as their actions will get in the way of your child's health.

In time, you will find that your support team isn't only there for your child but is also there for *you* and the rest of your family when you simply need someone to talk to or to lean on. In the most general terms, however, your support team is there to provide a solid foundation for you to begin taking charge of your child's health. If you or your child should ever fall, you can be assured that you'll never fall far without someone catching you and helping you back up. With a support team in place, you are ready to tackle the next step.

Communicate with Your Child

Angela, age thirty-one, is a single mother whose daughter, Carlie, was diagnosed with ADD/ADHD in the first grade. The diagnosis came as no surprise to Angela, because Carlie had problems with hostile, disruptive outbursts at school. Even though she knew that she would get Carlie back to school eventually, she hired a special-needs babysitter to take care of Carlie during the day while she was at the office. It didn't work. Carlie was restless and irritable and threw tantrums, and there wasn't enough time for Angela to set limits, let alone educate her. Where were all the joys of motherhood? she wondered.

Angela's situation is not an extreme example of something many parents of children with ADD/ADHD face. From the moment your child is diagnosed, you might operate in crisis mode and focus all your attention each day on urgent matters and emergencies rather than on long-term solutions. You may seem to be managing your life from crisis to crisis—dealing with each temper tantrum as it comes and each school disaster as it happens. You may feel constantly fatigued and unappreciated.

You probably haven't had the time to notice the ways in which the dialogue between you and your child has broken down. It's time to repair these communication lines and make sure your child understands what is happening to him or her and is actively involved in getting better.

Find a low-stress, quiet time for a casual family meeting. Frame the situation as it is—a family issue. If you allow all family members a chance to share their frustrations, your child will not feel singled out. Admit to and apologize for getting angry and impatient too quickly. Siblings can do the same. Then give the child a chance to talk with loving, supportive prompting. Don't use this informal meeting as an opportunity to talk about nutrition, exercise, and so on. There's plenty of time to discuss these issues at a later date.

Family conversations like these should always end with an assurance of everyone's care and love for one another, a renewal of the promise to work together to get the family back on track, and a reminder that frustrations like these should be spoken aloud calmly anytime they arise—not just in family meetings. One of the goals of these conversations should be to show everyone involved that this is a group project, that a fully operational support team has been assembled—and that everyone will do his or her part to help the situation.

Exercises like these are instrumental in the healing process and in opening up communication lines with the child with behavioral issues. When family activities thereafter—like dinnertime and playtime—can be identified as group projects, your ADD/ADHD child and his or her siblings will tend to have better attitudes about eating healthier foods at dinnertime that may not always taste as good as junk foods and about playing together outdoors instead of sitting in front of a television set.

In families in which the dynamic has become explosive and seriously damaged, it may be helpful to repair communication by holding a family meeting in the presence of a family therapist. Specialists in family dynamics are trained in steering conversations in healthy directions and curtailing hurtful rants or accusations. A therapist can work like a referee.

Discuss these ideas and set the precedent for healthy communication by resisting the urge to yell or scold, let alone humiliate or embarrass. Stay calm. The key to all of this is to avoid, as best you can, situations that are difficult and anxiety-provoking for your child and family. Avoid circumstances you know just won't work.

Educate Your Family and Friends

The family members and friends you've identified as members of your support team are those who have already demonstrated that they care deeply about the health of your child. Because of their compassion, they may be concerned when you tell them you're going to take an unconventional approach to treating ADD/ADHD.

Doctors and the media have helped to create the belief that the best way to treat ADD/ADHD is with stimulant medications, such as Ritalin or Adderall. These medications are often accompanied by a second medication (antidepressants or sedatives) to treat the side effects of the first medication. Your friends and family may not understand the plan to avoid, decrease, or eliminate these medications. Explain to them the side effects of these medications and the huge potential for curing ADD/ADHD naturally with great nutrition, exercise, sleep, and boundary-setting.

To further help your friends and family understand what you are doing, let them know that well-respected medical researchers and mainstream medical journals support your choice. There's a growing body of research that shows the link between a poor, sugar-laden diet and the exacerbation of ADD/ADHD symptoms. Please let them know that you're serious and need their help.

Don't let them make the mistake of feeding your child the sort of junk food that undermines your goals and your child's health. Make sure they recognize the importance of exercise for your child, so that they will plan physical activities for playdates rather than renting videos for the children to watch. Once they understand that this is a solid, intelligent, medical approach to the problem, they'll be more supportive and better equipped to help you reverse your child's ADD/ADHD.

Inform Your Child's Caregivers or School

Teachers are often the ones who bring the possibility of ADD/ADHD to the attention of parents for the first time, usually when the child is around five years old. Educators, along with the rest of us, may still think of drug treatments as the first option. Explain your plans to your child's teachers and discuss with them the severity of the problem. Tell them that you and your child need their help in not feeling pressured to change things overnight with drugs. It never hurts to ask for time and extra help.

Teachers will be able to watch for behavioral problems that may signal a lapse in your child's progress, which will need to be addressed at home. They can prove invaluable in helping to prevent lunchtime food trading. It is a good idea to follow up with teachers on a regular basis. All teachers should be happy to help you because they're familiar with the side effects associated with medications and the inconvenience and stigma that go along with taking a midday pill at school. If they are not happy to help you in this respect, it's time to find a new teacher who is willing to provide the support you need.

Set Up Successful Interactions
with Other Children

Realistically, your school administrators will be too busy with their various duties to moderate *all* of your child's interactions. On a similar note, it's of little benefit to the long-term development of your child if you must watch over all of his or her playdates. Your child's already leading a normal life, albeit with more interpersonal challenges than some of the other kids. It's really important for you to let your child continue to make his or her own way and grow into someone who is a good friend to others. As things get better, you'll keep testing the waters with more playdates and more social activities. As usual, be brief and clear as you discuss limits and boundaries with your child. Either avoid tricky situations or be ready to intervene should things get out of hand. Although you won't be able to shield your child from all the difficulties he or she will encounter in dealing with peers, there are certainly things you can do to maximize the chance for a successful interaction—namely, removing those things that you know trigger negative behaviors.

Along with clear limits and boundaries, diet is the key to mitigating ADD symptoms. For playdates at your house and other children's houses, talk to parents in advance. You may want to prepare your child's meals and snacks beforehand. If you do that, prepare enough for all the children who are going to be there so they can all eat together.

There will be setbacks in your child's interactions, and things may not go as smoothly as you like, but do not be discouraged! Keep things in perspective. Focus on all the things that go right and remember to reinforce and gently correct your child's behavior.

Address the Special Needs of Siblings

Siblings may have a difficult time adjusting to the changes you are making. The whole family is eating differently now. There is less time spent in front of the TV and playing video games. Things are changing, and siblings may be reluctant to participate in the family's new lifestyle.

The key to handling any tensions that may arise is to let your other children know that you don't expect them to respond "just right" every single time their brother or sister with ADD/ADHD annoys them. You'll find that sometimes—more often than not—you will have to separate siblings when things get really tense. One parent may have to take one child out to play in a park while the other parent takes the rest of the kids to a mall to blow off some steam. Friends and relatives can also help diffuse tense situations by taking one or more of your children for an outing in order to help things settle down.

Despite these (hopefully rare) tense days, coping with ADD/ADHD can bring out warm feelings and kindness in your children. You can use the condition as an opportunity to come together as a family. There's nothing sad about that!

6

Let's Behave!: Behavioral Therapy

We should never imply that children with ADD/ADHD are bad children. We need to think of their situation this way: their behavior is not working for them, nor is it working for anyone else. It doesn't allow them to form the relationships and friendships that they deserve, and it's keeping them from enjoying and contributing to the overall family harmony.

While we're doing everything else—eating well, exercising, and sleeping regularly—we need to also find ways to gradually but directly modify our child's behavior.

Time Off for Good Behavior

There is truth in the old adage that "You can catch more flies with honey than with vinegar"—especially in cases involving ADD/ADHD. Consider for a moment the number of mean and hurtful comments and negative reactions directed toward children with ADD/ADHD on a daily basis at school. These children tend to get more than their fair share of vinegar, and, even worse, they are probably used to it! Imagine how they will welcome kind, gentle behavior modification at home.

Behavioral therapy in children with ADD/ADHD must be, above all, a positive experience, because you can be certain that they've grown numb to being yelled at and punished. For behavioral therapy to be most effective, you need to approach it with the understanding that it is not merely the child's behavior that must be coaxed into change. If quick personal changes are to be made, we're the ones to make them. Our children can be expected to change only with our help and guidance.

Behavioral therapy doesn't need to involve a professional, although some families feel more comfortable when there is one involved. All you really need in order to enact positive behavioral changes in your child is creativity, patience, adaptability, and a positive attitude. A persistent, positive attitude will prove the most challenging, but again, as adults, we can do it, and our children will respond in kind.

We'll get into the fundamentals of traditional behavioral therapy and some innovative and effective methods to help your entire family. Later, we'll also explore cognitive behavioral therapy—a method of behavior modification that has grown in popularity as a positive way to bring about significant change in the lives of children coping with attention deficit and behavioral issues.

Behavioral Therapy Basics

Stella, a wonderful mother, had a domestic life that she was not proud of and a social life that was practically nonexistent. Her nine-year-old son, Malcolm, was a difficult little boy as a result of his ADD/ADHD, and the strain of raising him contributed to a rift between Stella and her husband that widened daily. Following a less-than-amicable divorce, she found herself in the role of single parent. Malcolm was already performing poorly at school and disrupting the class on a daily basis. He was benched at recess almost every single day for some classroom infraction. At least once a week, he was sent to the principal's office for especially disruptive classroom behavior (throwing things at other students, screaming at the teacher, or simply refusing to stay in his seat during class). The breakup of his parents' marriage and the subsequent destabilizing of his life only worsened his behavior at a time when Stella was at her most vulnerable.

In the evenings after work, Stella was too worn out to be on constant alert, but she had to be, anyway. Malcolm would break objects around the house with no apparent remorse, or would attempt to run out of the house when she wasn't looking. Worst of all, around bedtime, Malcolm would throw a nasty, prolonged, and loud tantrum, flinging himself to the ground and pounding and kicking and thrashing so violently that Stella was afraid he might hurt himself or even hurt her. When Malcolm threw these tantrums, Stella found that words and threats of punishment never helped. She would have to resort to restraining her son by holding his wrists or pinning him to the carpet until he tired himself out. Initially, she believed that if she did this often enough, Malcolm would learn that expending so much energy on struggling would be futile and that he eventually wouldn't bother.

But night after night, episode after episode, the tantrums continued until they became routine. On a good night, the episodes would last only a few minutes; on bad nights, they would last half an hour or more.

Stella came to me sad, depressed, and frustrated. She told me that there were many nights when she was ready to accept that Malcolm might remain absolutely incorrigible and could turn out to be a sociopath no matter what she did. We sat down together at first for a session without Malcolm present, and Stella described for me her situation in detail. When she finished, I was able to point out to her a pattern that changed her perspective of how Malcolm viewed the world and his place in it.

Malcolm's case of ADD/ADHD was real and pressing, and his temper, tantrums, and outbursts were certainly not his fault—nor were they Stella's. What was happening to Malcolm was something that involved everyone in his life—from his teachers to his classmates to his relatives. People reacted to Malcolm in the way that was natural to them; his disruptive behaviors were met with strong discouragement, and if these behaviors persisted, then protest would quickly turn into punishment. Malcolm was only doing what was natural to him, and people reacted in a way that was natural to them. He grew used to the entire process and became numb to punishment and immune to insult. In fact, he had come to expect them and accept them. Stella's suspicions were correct: Malcolm had incorporated tantrums and the resulting punishment into his daily routine.

To change Stella's focus, I had her tell me a few things Malcolm could do without any trouble. At first, she couldn't help but continue to list the things that Malcolm *couldn't* do yet: go to bed without a fuss, eat everything on his plate at meals, clean up after himself, and so forth. With encouragement, however, Stella admitted that one thing that Malcolm did automatically was dress himself in the morning. He seemed to enjoy the process of putting together his own outfits. The items of clothing rarely matched, and he left his drawers open and his room in disarray. But he never needed to be told to get dressed before school.

When Stella brought Malcolm in for his first session, I shook his hand warmly and enthusiastically and told him that I was happy to meet him. "Your mother has told me so many great things about you!" I exclaimed, and he was clearly surprised. When I complimented his unusual outfit (a T-shirt sporting an image of Homer Simpson and what looked like swim trunks), he beamed with pride.

We sat down together, and Stella and I folded our hands on the desk between us, leaning forward to begin the conversation. Although Malcolm's hyperactivity was manifesting itself as wildly kicking feet underneath the desk, he folded his hands as we were doing and remained seated for the duration of the session. In fact, other than the kicking, he was extremely well-behaved. Throughout our talk, neither Stella nor I scolded him or even turned our attention to the kicking.

Intrigued by the power and the possibilities of positive reinforcement, Stella was willing to change her perception and start giving positive behavioral therapy for her son a try. Once she saw the need for a change, all I had to do was offer occasional guidance. Stella managed to devise her own behavioral therapy at home based on some key principles and helpful pointers I gave her.

The basic principle is something that is already clear: punishment may discourage certain behaviors in the short run, but more often than not it will be ineffective in improving your child's behavior in the long run. Positive reinforcement and encouragement, respect and love, however, will do wonders.

Positive reinforcement can do the following:

1. Reverse the mentality in kids with ADD/ADHD that allows them to accept that they are "bad," as everyone seems to believe. It ends the vicious cycle.

2. Foster a happier home environment that puts everyone at greater ease and minimizes outbursts and frustration.

3. Allow a parent to feel that he or she is not, in fact, a bad parent who has to yell and punish all the time.

4. Be generally more rewarding and harmonizing in the long run for everyone in the family.

If you begin seriously evaluating where negativity has started to interfere with the happiness at home, you can be overwhelmed by its prevalence—and excited by all the areas in which you can try a more positive attitude. Getting started is easier than you would imagine.

The Project: Creating Structure and Shaping Goals

Children with attention deficit disorders can be surprisingly goal oriented. In fact, they can be accustomed to completing most tasks with determination and efficiency when they perceive that there is a clear structure to an activity. A recent five-year study conducted at Lehigh University, paid for by the National Institutes of Health, showed encouraging results. In the study, behavioral therapies that stressed consistent rules and routines, time limits for certain tasks, and more praise for good behavior than punishment for bad were applied to 135 preschoolers with severe ADD/ADHD. After a year, the children experienced a drop in problem behaviors and aggression by about 30 percent, with a corresponding 30 percent improvement in learning. This remarkable study was published in the September 2007 journal of the *National Association of School Psychologists*.

These results show that even though it may seem that many activities fail to hold the attention of children with ADD/ADHD, in truth they are capable of performing tasks with commitment and a surprising single-mindedness if some structure is supplied. They are much more likely to do well at a task for which they have a clear-cut goal or end point, and for which there is obvious evidence of their ongoing progress.

The challenge for you is to make improving behavior part of a larger project of self-improvement, with clear benchmarks along the way.

Suggestions follow in this chapter, but you can use your own imagination and parental intuition to custom-design a method for your own family.

The "Game" Method for Managing ADD/ADHD

One creative method suggested by many ADD/ADHD experts is to create a chart or a board game with spaces that players can advance along toward the finish line. To liven up the spirit of entertainment, you can use the game board of one of your child's favorite games or create your own based on a theme that you know your child will love. The idea is basically to enact an interesting, exciting game at home in which each member of the family gets a game piece that he or she can move forward a certain number of spaces every day for improving behavior. The behaviors or chores—and the corresponding number of spaces to advance for each—serve as the official rules of the game. Saying thank you when someone does something nice for you, for example, may allow a player to move ahead one space. Cleaning up an entire room advances a player three spaces, setting the table for the family two spaces, clearing your own plate after a meal one space, and so forth. When a player reaches the last space on the board game, he or she is rewarded.

There are several keys to ensuring that the game is a positive one. First, all family members should be players so that the child with ADHD does not feel like he or she is being singled out. The idea of a family-wide game can also inject a sense of fun and togetherness into daily life; these things could have been lost and sorely missed in families that have struggled with behavioral issues for a long time. Second, the game should have no losers. Even after one player reaches the finish line and moves his or her game piece to the first square on the board, the other players continue on their path toward the finish line. Therefore, no one can lose at the game. The players are not competing against one another; they just win at different times. The reward for a player reaching the last square should be something that the entire family can celebrate together—perhaps a night out at a restaurant of the winner's choice. Third, punishment should have no place in this game. If a child is forced to move a game piece backward along the board for bad behavior, then the game becomes simply another symbol of authority and enforcement for the child to reject or act out against.

Other Methods for Managing ADHD

If a daily game seems too complicated for your family, you can also choose a method that uses small incentives to encourage better behavior. Stickers or trading cards make good choices because they are inexpensive and yet very attractive and collectible to young children. Just as with the board game method, there should be a clear-cut list of behaviors that will bring rewards so that your child will know exactly what to do to earn them.

Keep in mind that any method that promotes improvement in behavior is most effective when there is a tangible representation of progress that a child can see with his or her eyes. It's a good idea to provide your child with a card box, a sticker book, a notebook, or anything else that he or she can use to contain the rewards and to see how much has been accumulated over time. A collection of rewards earned over a long period is a great reminder of the strides the child has made and can be

Behavioral Modification Programs for Purchase

Certain companies that specialize in creating educational products have designed their own programs to aid in behavior modification in children with ADD/ADHD. Here are some that are currently available.

Magnetic Responsibility Chart, $24.99

This fold-open chart includes 134 wooden magnetic pieces that depict various chores, behaviors, and rewards. Four blank pieces are included so that your family can personalize the chart.

Behavior Beasts Child Behavior Management System, $29.95

Through the use of fictional characters named Messy, Grubby, Stingy, Noisy, Nasty, and Fussy, this innovative program uses a game board, cassettes, stickers, a poster, and a rewards system to teach and encourage improved behavior in young children.

What-a-Kid Coupon Books, $19.95

This book offers more than 128 colorful coupons to motivate your kids for doing good work, completing tasks, or behaving well. This product makes it easy to present rewards the instant you catch your child doing something that deserves commending.

These products are all available at www.WeBehave.com.

very encouraging in times when the child doubts himself or herself. And don't forget the major benchmarks! The incentive to behave well will be greater if, along the way, a certain number of stickers or cards earned means that the child earns a bigger prize—a desired toy, a trip to an amusement park, or the child's choice of a favorite dish for dinner.

I'm very familiar with the school of thought and the many books that say that rewarding children for improved behavior isn't good for them. I couldn't disagree more. In the real world, improving behavior at a job, in school, or anywhere else results in job promotions, good grades, friendships, and more. As we create this framework for helping our kids with ADD/ADHD, we should certainly incorporate real-world strategies, including tangible rewards to go with our words of praise and our children's feelings of accomplishment.

For the Parent

Whether you choose to use an ongoing board game to encourage improving behavior or a steady stream of incentives in your form of behavioral therapy, the purpose is to get your child to associate good behavior with positive feelings so that it becomes second nature for him or her to act appropriately in all situations without your prompting or urging. As long as you keep in mind the importance of staying positive in your messages to your child, you can devise your own method of treatment at home, purchase a prepackaged behavioral modification program kit available through companies that design educational products, or hire a professional behavioral therapist to help oversee the process.

No matter which method you choose, the first step to take before you embark on any effort to modify your child's behavior is to look at your own.

How often do you react in a negative way to the actions of your child? How often do you resort to punishment rather than explanations when your child misbehaves? How often do you compliment your child?

You can catch yourself in your negative reactions now that you are aware of them. The next time you ask your child to complete a task and come back to find it only partially completed (or even barely started), try to respond with a positive comment about the work he or she has already done, and then say how proud you will be when you see the task completed. If your child performs poorly on a school assignment, point out the questions or problems he or she was able to complete correctly, and extend some heartfelt congratulations.

You will be pleasantly surprised when you discover that your child is more capable of self-motivation than you ever could have imagined, as he or she responds to positive reinforcement, encouraging words, and tangible rewards rather than yelling, nagging, or punishment. When you consider that children with ADD/ADHD have particularly low tolerance for frustration or disappointment, then you can truly understand what little good punishment does to help a child with ADD/ADHD, and why encouragement and reinforcement are the better choices by far.

Positivity should always have a place in your parenting methods when you are raising a child with behavioral issues, but remember that another important element that must be part of your child's life is structure. A behavioral therapy that focuses on the pragmatic ways of dealing with ADD/ADHD has grown out of this concept. It's known as cognitive behavioral therapy.

Cognitive Behavioral Therapy

You already know that of the many things that can complicate recovery from ADD/ADHD, one of the most troubling has nothing to do with brain chemistry or genetics at all. The greatest roadblock for a child with ADD/ADHD symptoms can be lack of self-esteem. In other words, the disorder can lead to the development of psychological problems that are difficult to correct with only words of encouragement and a sprinkling of sincere compliments.

Children with ADD/ADHD have it rough, and sometimes there is only so much a parent can do to undo the damage that is done outside of the home. These children have been singled out in class, ostracized by their classmates, and sometimes even ridiculed by former friends. And what's worse, they might even accept all the mean remarks about their character or intellect as the truth, no matter what their parents say to the contrary.

Self-doubt and defeatism make everything that much harder. They might be some of the biggest obstacles you'll face when trying to conquer a disorder as challenging and frustrating as ADD/ADHD. There are no medicines that are designed to reverse low self-esteem. (Okay, actually, in some ways there are: children on stimulant medication for ADD/ADHD very often require antidepressants to combat certain side effects of their primary medication. How can anybody possibly think that this is a good answer to the problem, let alone the best answer?) The cure for this is a gradual sort of therapy in which love and support are the main treatments. If you have removed negativity from your family life and are taking steps to encourage good behavior at home, you're already doing a lot to make life easier for your child. However, even as your child's behavior improves, negative feelings about himself or herself may remain. This is where cognitive behavioral therapy can prove useful.

Cognitive Behavioral Therapy Defined

Cognitive behavioral therapy (CBT) is a treatment that is designed to help people identify and become conscious of the negative thoughts and feelings that are keeping them from success in their daily lives. Children and adults who use CBT are coached to make concrete, observable changes to the way they see themselves and go about doing their daily tasks. As the name implies, there are two components to this form of therapy. The "cognitive" part involves identifying the negative thinking that is having a disruptive effect on the patient's life. The "behavior" part of the therapy involves adjusting behavior to systemically squash destructive thoughts and patterns that get in the way of accomplishing goals—from the immediate and mundane to the long term and grand.

This therapy is designed to be orderly and efficient, so progress can be traced, goals can be set and met, and children with ADD/ADHD can be provided with a concrete and much-needed sense of accomplishment.

Thinking, Feeling, Doing

Whether you decide to use the help of a professional cognitive behavioral therapist or decide to apply cognitive techniques to the way you go about tackling your child's ADD/ADHD, actual treatment begins when you show your child that his or her biggest roadblock in all things is negative thinking. Your child will be amazed at what can be accomplished once that roadblock is removed.

You can ask the following questions to help your child reach this conclusion:

- How do you feel when you are trying to do something that is hard?
- Do you ever feel like giving up even before you try?
- Can you remember a time when you tried to do something that was hard, and actually did it?
- How did you feel before you did it?
- How did you feel after?
- Did you know that *everyone* has trouble doing things correctly when they are stressed?
- Did you know that everything is easier to do if you just remember to stay positive?
- Did you know that there are no hardships in life for which there are no solutions?

To really convince children that negative thinking is their worst enemy, it helps to assure them of their great capability and their many great abilities. The very basic principle of CBT is that someone with ADD/ADHD can take control of his or her thoughts (and actions) and then behave with a clear mind.

CBT is not psychotherapy. It does not rely on ongoing analysis of the problem and constant discussions. Instead, CBT encourages children to face their challenges with confidence, set goals, and achieve them. We start our children with small, daily tasks at first and then build to bigger, longer-term goals.

Each day, you and your child set clear-cut goals that must be met by the day's end. These goals can be as simple as making a bed, finishing breakfast and cleaning up, finishing homework, and completing an exercise routine in a certain length of time. Each one should have a realistic time limit (you should set the time limits at first, because children with ADD/ADHD typically underestimate the time it will take to do something, and then become discouraged when something seems to take longer than they thought it would). The tasks can be simple, because the ultimate goal won't be finishing off the entire list, but rather using these tasks as an exercise in suppressing negative mind-sets and keeping thoughts realistic throughout the day.

Create a schedule on paper or on a computer, and help your child stick to it. The benefit of this strategy of CBT is that your child can track his or her progress, and every task completed is a concrete accomplishment. You can mark off each task as it is completed or, if the list is on paper, you can add a creative and motivational touch by placing a sticker next to each completed item. Suddenly, tasks have structure and meaning and end points. Previously, they might have looked like a mountain of disorganized, discouraging challenges.

As success increases day after day, and accomplishments are recorded, negative feelings and stress dissipate, and your child starts to develop a goal-oriented, optimistic outlook on daily challenges. With this boost in your child's self-esteem, weekly goals can be added, followed by monthly goals, and then long-term goals that have open-ended deadlines. The key to success in each of these is showing your child that every challenge and every problem can be broken up into smaller, much more manageable parts. Everything becomes possible, not *im*possible.

Working with a Professional

Depending on your confidence in your own coaching skills, you may choose to hire a professional cognitive behavioral therapist to guide your child in this therapy.

A professional therapist can identify your child's specific attention span from the outset and offer a more realistic assessment of what he or she can accomplish in the way of individual tasks. From there, the therapist can set a schedule for expanding this attention span by gradually incorporating more challenging and time-consuming tasks into your child's daily schedule.

Cognitive behavioral therapists also have some tricks of their trade that work particularly well with children. They can show you how to make this form of treatment fun and rewarding for the whole family.

A therapist can aid your child in planning weekly and longer-term goals that can be accomplished between meetings and speak as an authority with your child about his or her successes. The therapist can help assess what went wrong whenever performance falls short. The therapist can also candidly discuss with you things about your child's thoughts and feelings that he or she may not be willing to tell you for fear of disappointing you.

A professional cognitive behavioral therapist can be a trusted friend, confidant, and ally to call when you and your child run into snags at home.

Success Is the Best Medicine

You will find that ADD/ADHD is so much easier to handle once children develop a positive attitude about treatment and an optimistic view of their future success as they rid themselves of their most troublesome symptoms. Your child will be more willing to try those things that previously cast a shadow of self-doubt, and he or she will be a healthier, happier individual for it.

CBT fosters the organizational and planning skills that can make all the difference in the life of a child with ADD/ADHD. These skills can lead to constant success all the way into adulthood and a higher degree of self-confidence and rational optimism. In the end, there is nothing as effective as teaching children that they can succeed.

The Final Word on Behavioral Therapy

There is a whole world of methods available to parents who are concerned about their child's behavior, whether or not he or she has ADD/ADHD. With the application of structure, a positive attitude, plenty of love and support, creativity, respect, and adaptability, these methods will work for you and for your child. You can devise your own unique program, or you can use a method you read about in a book. Or you can use a method that has been designed for you by a professional. Overall, you can view behavioral therapy as a means by which children can be encouraged to consider the benefits of behaving a certain way before they act, rather than simply to react as their emotions would have them. And if you really think about it, this is essentially how most of us get through our days behaving appropriately in each situation we encounter. Children with ADD/ADHD just need a little more practice at this. With help and training, there is no reason that they can't overcome their symptoms.

7

Refocusing Your Child's Energy

During my office day, I see tired children and tired parents. And sometimes they see a tired doctor. All of us are enthusiastic and even passionate about things in life, but it's pretty darn hard to be passionate about things when you haven't gotten a good night's sleep. And it might be hard for children to maintain their enthusiasm for real life when they can get lost in the fantasy worlds—often violent ones— of video games and television shows. Refocusing your child's energy involves making sure that the energy is there and available. As we've discussed already, great nutrition makes a huge difference, and in this chapter I'd like to take a hard look at the issue of sleep. As I've mentioned earlier, I'm amazed at the number of people who just don't know why they're tired. I try not to be abrupt with them when I tell them that they just need more sleep.

I strongly recommend team sports for all the children in my practice. What I've found is that the children who pull away most strongly from basketball, volleyball, and soccer are the children for whom these team sports will be the most beneficial. I think that individual sports, such as martial arts, dancing, and singles tennis, are wonderful, but there's no substitute for the cooperation that children learn on the soccer field and on the basketball court. They learn that there will be some days and some games where they're the center of attention and other times when they're expected to be good strong members of the team. These lessons are particularly important for children with attention deficit problems.

The Importance of Sleep

School starts too early, and homework ends too late.

In some communities, this is only applicable to kids in middle school and up. But in some communities, kindergarten starts very early in the morning, and who on earth invented homework for first and second graders?

Children need the proper amount of sleep. For younger children, this usually means between ten and twelve hours a night. Even for teenagers, conventional medical wisdom is that they need ten hours sleep for optimal health. We adults have infused our culture with an absurd pride in sleeping less, thinking that it means we've accomplish more. While this is debatable in adults, for children, nothing could be further from the truth. Medical research has shown that everything, from academic and athletic success to driving skills, is adversely affected by lack of sleep.

When I do checkups, I sometimes joke with the older kids and say things like, "How much sleep does an eight-year-old or a ten-year-old or a twelve-year-old need? Let me tell you how you'll know. If you're tired, you need more sleep."

If your child is an active, engaged, happy child who gets enough rest, he or she certainly won't voluntarily waste energy on outbursts or tantrums. To make sure that your child *does* have enough energy to get through the day and to make the most of his or her waking hours, you must enforce and encourage good sleep habits. There's nothing wrong with creating and sticking to a strict bedtime.

Any growing child who isn't getting enough sleep is jeopardizing his or her development, but a sleep-deprived ADD/ADHD child is more likely to backslide and experience increased symptoms. *Any child* who isn't well rested will exhibit behavior problems. However, ADD/ADHD sufferers, more than other children, are in particular danger of losing control from lack of sleep.

It bears repeating: how much sleep does your child need? For preschoolers, it can be as much as twelve to thirteen hours a day, and as much as nine to ten hours for preteens. It is rare that any child can maintain balanced mental and physical health on less than eight hours of sleep a night.

Good healthy sleep depends on sleep cycles. Research has shown that normal growth, development, and alertness can be greatly aided by long, normal sleep cycles. I don't believe in sleep schedules for newborns and babies or even toddlers. But I tell all parents that from age three, children need to have a certain bedtime. I encourage parents to have lots of nighttime contact with their babies. I encourage them to be flexible when their toddlers need them in the middle of the night. But I also encourage them to promote good, long sleep intervals in school-age children. Activities before bedtime should be relaxing to allow a child to "turn off" the buzz of the day. If there's a night-light in the bedroom, it should be very dim, and children should not learn to fall asleep to the sound of a television set or a radio. The bedroom should be dark and quiet.

If your child isn't sleeping well or getting enough sleep, you need to establish a firm schedule and a daily routine you're prepared to stick to, with fixed times for getting to bed and waking up. When you first set a bedtime, you're going to encounter a lot of resistance and maybe even some whining and groaning. Being sent to bed before they really want to go to sleep may feel like punishment to many children. The trick is to create an enjoyable bedtime ritual with a series of events that you can set into motion each night. For example, you can read a book to your child right before bed. Follow this with a special bedtime song, a hug, and a kiss before tucking your child in for the night. Bedtime can easily be transformed from something to be dreaded to a warm, loving event that ends the day.

Once your child is under the covers, you must be firm. It's amazing how many children get "really hungry" just as the lights are being turned out. Your child may say something like, "Mom, I'm not asking for cookies. I just want a bowl of oatmeal." Here's what I recommend: on that first night, give your child the oatmeal and explain that you will incorporate the oatmeal into the bedtime ritual, but once the lights go out, he or she can't ask to be let out of bed for anything else. Try to make as few exceptions as possible. Of course, be understanding about the need to go to the bathroom or to get a glass of water, but be careful about letting this slide into an easily exploited set of loopholes. It's important to persist even though you might experience some trouble getting your child to fall asleep at first. It could take a few weeks or longer for your child to get used to the routine, but eventually your child's sleep pattern will change. He or she will start to fall asleep at the bedtime you set as long as you're firm, respectful, and loving. A good night's sleep gives you a well-rested child who will have the energy to have fun and succeed at school, at home, and in all areas of his or her life.

A Case of Misdirected Passion

Suk-yi Mun and her husband were Korean immigrants who were raising their son, Jae, in a California suburb. Both parents had grown up in South Korea, where academics were more demanding than in the United States. In a session together, Suk-yi and her husband said that despite the difficulty level of the school curriculum, neither of them was a particularly bad student (although neither excelled, either), and this was why they were so confused over how their son could do so poorly in school.

Jae was in the sixth grade and extremely introverted. Since he was never disruptive, his teachers never had any reason to complain about his behavior or even to notice him in a classroom full of faces. However, when the class was given timed assignments, the teacher reported that Jae would apparently "blank out" and stare endlessly at his paper, finally turning in partially completed essays when the time expired.

In our session, it was revealed quickly that Jae loved violent computer games—particularly the ones that allowed him to interact with other players over the Internet. His parents had noticed his love for these games early on and had been extremely vigilant about restricting the amount of time he was allowed to play them to a maximum of two hours a day. They also enforced a very strict policy of finishing homework before bedtime, and in this rule they were absolute and unbending. As a result, sometimes when Jae worked at an especially slow pace, he wouldn't be able to go to bed until midnight or later.

In addition to his obvious lack of sleep, Jae's love of computer games was an area in which I felt I needed to probe further. I asked him whether he thought often about these games when he wasn't playing them and how much he thought about the games after his two-hour gaming sessions ended. The answer to both of these questions was "a lot"—which he admitted with great hesitation and sheepishness.

A short lesson was in order for the entire family to understand their current situation more fully and so that Jae wouldn't be heaped with self-inflicted blame and guilt upon returning home. Suk-yi and her husband obviously loved Jae and were very supportive of him and concerned about his future, but the strictness with which they ran their household had created a tense environment in which—even without yelling or punishment—Jae was always sorely aware of his failures.

I asked Suk-yi and her husband if either of them had struggled with learning at all in school, and they both denied having had any real trouble. They did, however, say that other students had been "naturally smarter" than they were and that their inability to excel was never because of a failure to complete homework.

I suggested to them that perhaps their inability to excel was not a matter of intellect, but of a slight and latent case of ADD/ADHD in one or both of them that had never showed itself so fully as to disrupt their lives significantly. In the South Korean school system, where everything was structured well and order was upheld by teachers, and where the diet generally included far less processed junk, they were exposed to no triggers that would have brought out or exacerbated their ADD/ADHD.

Jae was growing up in a vastly different world. His ADD/ADHD had likely been triggered—and then exacerbated daily—by his video game playing. I guessed that he was also snacking on junk foods as he played. Under normal circumstances for most children, gaming or television watching in moderation is perfectly healthy. For a child with ADD/ADHD, however, the effects are more detrimental, to varying degrees depending on the severity of the disorder.

Many studies conducted over the last decade have exposed the correlation between the rapid rise of ADD/ADHD in children and the sheer glut of electronic entertainment available to kids today. These studies suggest that prolonged or regular video game playing or television watching can affect and significantly alter cognitive patterns, especially in young children whose minds are still in early developmental stages. Electronic entertainment is designed to provide continuous stimulation, and game and program developers have steadily become better at it. Over the years, the action in video games has grown more intense, and television shows for children now pack as many flashing colors, quick cuts, and consecutive action sequences in their time slot as possible. The result for children is that they never have to focus on any one scene for long in television shows; in the case of video games, quick and often repetitive reactions are rewarded with points, with enemies destroyed, and with objects collected.

Regular exposure to electronic entertainment results in shortened attention spans and heightened impatience in real-life situations when actions and efforts don't yield instantaneous, physical rewards.

In Jae's case, his parents had been right to make sure that his gaming took place in moderation. However, what they hadn't factored in was that the daily gaming session disrupted his entire day. In the hours prior to gaming, he was distracted by his anticipation. He usually rushed to his computer immediately upon returning home from school. After he'd played his games for two straight hours, his mind would be racing so quickly with the flashing images and the excitement that he couldn't reasonably be expected to focus on his homework for some time. The junk food, of course, wasn't helping. Meanwhile, his attention span was growing shorter, and his late nights and self-inflicted sleep deprivation were causing him to be exhausted during the day, when his school assignments required his attention.

As a first step, I advised the Mun family to rework the schedule so that Jae got some outdoor exercise and fresh air after returning home from school. This way, he'd be able to work out the tension built up from having to sit for so many hours at a desk, and the physical activity could refresh him and get his brain to work at its optimum, when all the endorphins were flowing freely. After exercise time would be time for homework. To foster an atmosphere that would aid him in his concentration, I suggested that Suk-yi prepare a nutritious snack for Jae to nibble on as "brain food" while working and to set up a designated work area that was comfortable and well-lit—and, at the same time, removed from the sight of distractions (like the computer). Computer gaming would have to be pushed back as an activity only to be enjoyed after homework was completed, and then never past a designated bedtime. Jae needed to get enough hours of sleep to be fresh and receptive at school the next day.

The ultimate goal, however, was to move computer gaming to the weekends and even to phase it out entirely. Jae's gaming addiction wouldn't serve him in the long run and had the potential to cripple him academically along the way. I encouraged the family to help Jae find a passion toward which he could redirect his energy.

This, of course, was in addition to a structured diet prescribed by my ADD/ADHD cure.

The Mun family, fortunately, were able to make the changes quickly and with clear results. The home-cooked meals they ate together were considerably more healthful than typical American meals. They merely had to start leaving out ingredients that included sugar, dairy, or wheat. The junk foods that Jae grabbed when he was hungry were thrown out. Jae's workspace moved from the desk in his room (where the computer was) to the kitchen table, where Suk-yi could track his progress and refresh his snack plate. Perhaps most beneficial to Jae was that his family installed a basketball hoop in the backyard so that he could shoot hoops after school, and his father began taking him out on weekends and on some weeknights to golf courses and driving ranges, where Jae began to develop a passion for the sport and an even closer bond with his father. Soon after, he joined a soccer team and started getting to know and interacting with a larger group of friends (his teammates) as well. Computer games were soon pushed to the background, and the Mun family was happy to report that the addiction was more or less broken and Jae's schoolwork was showing marked improvement in two months' time.

Jae is one of many bright kids whom I've had the pleasure of meeting whose life, unfortunately, was being consumed by video games. The dangerous combination of instant gratification and continuous overstimulation can be especially alluring to children who become bored easily in their daily lives (as is the case with children with ADD/ADHD). However, in the case of electronic entertainment, giving children what they want would be giving them precisely what they don't need. The truth is that *all* children—not just children with attention deficit or behavioral disorders—have untapped reservoirs of energy. One of the most important things you can do as a parent to fortify their mental health and to ensure their greatest developmental progress is simply to make sure their energy gets directed into all the right places.

Refocusing Your Child's Energy

If you think of your own life, chances are you can identify several ways in which you are constantly distracted by all the new technology that has entered into it. How many times do you break from a larger task to check your e-mail every day? How many Web sites do you visit daily, and how many seconds do you let a page load before you grow impatient and click out of it? How often do you drive and talk on your cell phone at the same time?

Some social scientists have pointed out that many adults these days live an ADD lifestyle. We split our focus because we have to, because all this technology allows us to multitask, and because the huge volume of work that we are expected to do in our many roles demands it. Despite technology's claim to make life easier and more efficient, many of us find ourselves more hectic, hurried, and harried. And when we aren't hard at work, today's multimedia environment—with its endless array of cell phones, portable music and video players, electronic games, and home entertainment centers—provides all of us with a continuous stream of distractions. Now imagine the effect of this on those for whom ADD is not a lifestyle choice but a real disorder. For children with ADD, whether the inattentive or hyperactive type, digital entertainment makes their condition worse and sabotages efforts to control the symptoms.

The truth is that no matter how technology enhances our performance at work or our leisure at home, people who are successful know how to complete tasks—no matter how challenging or time-consuming the tasks may be. We all have to identify the things we think are important and then figure out how to focus our energies into them. We all struggle to learn this, but those with ADD/ADHD have an even harder time.

For a parent, your first obligation is to make sure that your child is happy and healthy. Granted, some would argue that homework takes away from happiness, but there are healthy ways to do homework, too. Homework shouldn't interfere with sleep or exercise. With this policy in mind, you'll find that good amounts of sleep and exercise will actually help your child with homework! And once your children start facing school and homework with high levels of energy, fueled by their healthy lifestyles, they'll learn how to care about and *enjoy* learning.

Fostering a Passion for Learning

As you make the necessary adjustments to your child's diet, you'll be encouraged as you see his or her concentration levels steadily improve. At this point, you'll be able to begin helping your child develop something that has likely been placed on the back burner because of the more pressing behavioral problems: good study habits.

We've all regarded schoolwork as a chore at one point or another in our lives. However, for a child to see schoolwork and homework as bothersome and tedious just won't help his or her future success in high school, college, and beyond. In getting your recovering ADD/ADHD child to enjoy schoolwork, you must first have the proper attitude and then you must pass this attitude on to your child. The improper way to look at schoolwork would be to encourage your child to just "suck it up and do it" or "take it like a man (or woman)," as if schoolwork were something very unpleasant. You'll get the best and longest-lasting results if you can teach your child to enjoy learning new things and to avoid hours-long study binges. There are more efficient, less tiresome, and more fun ways to do study and learn. The following basic steps can help your child foster a love of learning.

Create a Pleasant Work Environment

Homework can be unbearable to our children when they are surrounded by reminders of the purely fun things they could be doing instead. This is why it is important that your child's workspace be away from the sight of televisions, computers, media players, and video game consoles— basically anything that will tempt your child to drop his or her pen or pencil and pick up a remote control or video game controller instead.

Some parents allow their children to do their homework on the carpet in front of the television set or on their beds with their MP3 players or CD players blasting music into their ears. You know that they couldn't possibly be absorbing much from their homework and their textbooks with these distractions. You know that it will take them twice as long to finish (which means twice the amount of time sitting, lying down, or otherwise being cooped up indoors and inactive). You have to remove these distractions from the picture. Your child is probably not going to like these changes at first, and he or she will let you know it. However, you can make things easier by setting up a work area that is comfortable and to his or her liking.

Designating one spot in your house as the official workspace is important for several reasons. First, it creates structure; your child will understand that when he or she is in the workspace, it is time to work. Second, you can control the presence and proximity of distractions and reduce the hassle of finding lost assignments and school supplies when all the work is done in one place.

Make sure the workspace is well lit—preferably with a white-light lightbulb; it's been shown that yellow light is harsher on the eyes and can therefore cause sleepiness. Anything else that you can do to make the workspace peaceful and comfortable can help your child want to stay in it. Good ventilation, a window with a view of outside greenery (but not of the street, where constant activity amounts to constant distraction), or playing soft classical music are all great ideas.

Set a Work Schedule

If you allow children to mix work time with playtime, you are inviting them to invent their own distractions. This is why it is important to fix certain hours of the day as official homework time. The best time for children to begin homework is right after they've had some exercise, when they have a good supply of oxygen circulating through their systems and their brain is prepped for concentration. Make it clear that they shouldn't leave the table until they have finished their assignment, or until it's time to have dinner.

A common problem with children recovering from ADD/ADHD is being intimidated by a large volume of work that sits, undone, before them. Setting up a work schedule and breaking assignments down into small parts is the best way to make homework appear manageable. To start, it's a good idea to review with your child the assignments that need to be done for the day and to create a checklist. If you can come up with an interesting way to check off the items on the list (with stickers, colorful pens, or another fun method), this may provide extra motivation for your child to get through the individual items more methodically. Additionally, if there is a reward waiting when the homework is completed, like a few more hours of playtime, that is all the more incentive for your child to work as hard and with as much concentration as he or she can.

Feed Their Brains

We've already discovered that food can affect mood, motivation, and mental health in the long run. The good news is that the proper food can also provide great energy boosts right now.

There is a reason people get the munchies when they are studying hard or really straining their brains. The brain is a highly metabolically active organ. While it is operating at full power, it is hungry for the right kinds of fuel. If fed properly when it is at work, the human mind can sharpen its memory, enhance motivation, improve reaction time, and cope with stress much more efficiently.

Omega-3 fatty acids are especially conducive to brain function because they prime the outer membranes on brain cells to receive signals from nerves more efficiently, thereby maximizing learning potential. Foods rich in omega-3 fatty acids are good snacks during work time. These include walnuts, cooked soybeans (edamame), strawberries, and anything with raw tofu in it. B vitamins have a similar effect, while also boosting energy. These vitamins are found in abundance in citrus fruits like oranges and grapefruit.

Offer Your Help; Participate

Children recovering from their ADD/ADHD symptoms will still be struggling with their homework, so it's key to let them know that they don't have to struggle alone. Check in with them once in a while to monitor their progress (without hovering). Offer help on any difficult problems.

Remind them that they have support whenever they need it and that no matter what the assignment is, they are smart enough to do it.

With younger children, it might be necessary to sit with them and act enthused about their homework. Younger kids have an extraordinary and endearing ability to match their moods and their level of happiness to those around them. If you act eager to learn, they will, too. Eventually, you'll want to teach them to work on their own. In the meantime, modeling the behavior you want them to eventually emulate can prove invaluable at the very beginning.

Show Genuine Interest

Learning from books is important, but up until the moment when your child started recovering from ADD/ADHD, he or she was struggling to learn how to behave well first. As your child's moods improve and behaving well becomes a natural function of his or her brain chemistry normalizing, it is time to communicate to your child the importance of education. The easiest way to do this is to show genuine interest in their education.

At dinnertime, before bedtime, or on the car ride home from school, make sure to ask your child, "What interesting things did you learn today?" and then take care to show true interest. If you contribute your own knowledge to the subject, your child will have something interesting to say in class the following day. This will get your child in the habit of participating in class discussions, and he or she will become more confident. Remember that your enthusiasm is contagious. The more impressed you are with his or her learning, the more impressed your child will be with the power of knowledge.

Encourage, Encourage, Encourage

Children who have low self-esteem, as do many who have ADD/ADHD, often end up on the dangerous path of looking for ways in which they are not as good or as smart as others. You can bet that there is no one better at discouraging a child than himself or herself.

In my practice, I've discovered that by the time children are seven or eight years old, they are fully capable of knowing when they've failed, and they are fully capable of understanding that their peers and superiors are angry and disappointed with them. They know what getting an *F* on a report card means as opposed to getting an *A*. In short, they are harsher in their judgments of themselves than you could ever be.

School grading systems are especially unsympathetic to the learning differences and obstacles that are unique to each child; and so where the system fails, you must guard your child against the damage that it can do to his or her progress.

The more effort your child has been putting into improving grades, the more hurt he or she will be by a less-than-satisfactory one. The child certainly won't need you to act disappointed in him or her to feel any worse. You can encourage positive thinking and promote higher self-esteem by treating each disappointing grade as an opportunity to show your child how to look on the bright side and to point out the ways in which his or her efforts have paid off. As clichéd as the concept of an "A for effort" is, you should stress this idea with your child while also doing the following:

- Pointing out all the things he or she did right on an assignment.

- Discussing the simple things he or she can do to improve the grade.

- Encouraging him or her to ask for help when needed.

- Reassuring him or her that progress comes slowly, and that any improvement—great or small—is something to be proud of.

Directing children's focus to their schoolwork is important not just for their future success in the academic and professional worlds but also for conditioning their minds to remain focused on a task, no matter how challenging or endless it may seem.

Of course, we all know the saying that begins "All work and no play . . ." After children are on the right track with their schoolwork, it's time to find other areas into which they can funnel their extra energy.

Discovering Interests and Cultivating Passions

For parents who are in the habit of relying on digital entertainment to keep their hyperactive or inattentive children occupied, the thought of setting limits and restricting exposure to television, video games, MP3 players, and computers may be a little scary. "What are they going to do with their time, then?" you'll ask. You may even wonder if what they'll do with their time will cut into *your* time.

It's true, when they're first told they will have to cut down on gaming and television watching—even when they're done with all their home-work—our kids grow upset and assume that they are being punished for no apparent reason. The backlash can be unpleasant for everyone. The key to minimizing the trauma is to simultaneously (and tactfully!) dis-cuss, introduce, and explore constructive activities as replacements to smooth the transition. If you only do some digging, you'll find more entertaining and enjoyable activity options that you'll know what to do with. You'll easily find one that your child with ADD/ADHD will want to pour his or her energy and concentration into.

Identifying Their Passion

Replacing empty, time-wasting activities with constructive ones is sim-ilar to swapping junk foods for nourishing food. You'd never expect the great difference that comes from just a few simple adjustments. When children regularly escape into sedentary modes of entertainment such as television watching and video gaming to keep their minds occupied, their true passions remain undiscovered. Helping your child to discover these passions can be a rewarding journey and an unforgettable parent-ing adventure. Here are a few tips to get you started.

- Begin the dialogue with your child sometime before you start tak-ing the steps to restrict or cut down on their gaming or television-watching time. Find a time when conversation would be most natural, such as on a long car ride or at the dinner table. You can start by mentioning an activity that you've always wanted to do, and never got the opportunity to try. "You know," you can say, "when I was your age, I wanted more than anything to _____." If it's something your child can never imagine you doing (like starting a rock band, or becoming an Olympic athlete), it's all the better for prompting interest in the conversation. No matter how you bring up the subject, eventually you'll swing the conversation around to your child and ask if there has ever been activity or hobby he or she has wanted to try. You may be surprised at what they have to say, and you may not be. Either way, you'll have your first clue into a healthy activity that can substitute for the unhealthier ones.

- You can gather plenty of clues about what your child may be interested in by observing the types of video games or television shows they prefer. Kids who like fighting games may have built-in enthusiasm for martial arts classes (where, by the way, they'll learn discipline, not violence or aggression). If your child likes musical programs, it might be worth investing in a karaoke machine or a music teacher to fine-tune his or her musical talent. Sometimes, it takes a bit more exploration beyond the obvious to figure out what might interest the child. If your child enjoys movies like *The Little Mermaid*, you can suggest swimming as a fun activity. If he or she is enamored of *Harry Potter*, you can't easily enroll your child in sorcery, witchery, or wizardry classes, but you can certainly suggest football or soccer, games upon which "Quidditch"—the fictional airborne game enjoyed by the characters in the book—is based. A little imagination and correlative thinking will serve you well in discovering an activity that your child can get enthused over. (See the Suggested Activities sidebar on page 170 for ideas.)

- Participate. If your child has struggled with ADD/ADHD for any amount of time, he or she may lack friends with whom to share new interests, activities, or hobbies. Your participation will do a lot in helping your child to develop a budding interest into a full-fledged passion or hobby. You can strengthen the bond between you and your child, which may have been strained while you were trying unsuccessfully to manage his or her symptoms in the past. Your willingness to participate in the newfound interests of your child will assure your child that what he or she is doing is "right" and worth pursuing with everything they've got.

Indulging Their Passion

You may have your own ideas of the best and healthiest activities for your child, but keep in mind that the choice isn't yours to make, and it shouldn't be. An interest or an activity that children invest themselves in will have the longest shelf life if they feel the closest possible connection to it. That means the idea should be theirs.

Unless the activity is completely objectionable and dangerous, you should try your best to be open-minded about what your child suggests. Be fully prepared to engage in the activity yourself with enthusiasm. Even if the interest is there, children struggling with ADD/ADHD may still experience difficulty with their focus on it. The best way to make sure this doesn't happen is to lead by example. This requires that you—and better, the whole family—understand their interests and take part in them to motivate the child to keep at it.

Being involved in your child's activities, interests, and passions doesn't require *direct* involvement. Simply being a presence, a fan, an advocate, or a spectator can do a lot toward creating a sense of unity and support. If your child chooses a sport as an activity, you can plan whole days around sporting events. Bring your spouse and other children along to cheer, and pack a picnic to eat at the park afterward, with special celebratory (and healthy) treats to enjoy no matter the outcome of the game.

Suggested Activities

There are plenty of ways you can clue yourself into your child's interests or potential passions from the types of media they are drawn to. Below are some suggested activities. You can have your child write a check mark next to the ones that he thinks he'll enjoy, and you'll have an excellent starting point.

Acting	Martial arts
Baseball	Model plane/car/ship building
Basketball	Playing an instrument
Biking	Puppet shows
Card tricks	Reading
Dancing	Singing
Drawing or painting	Soccer
Football	Swimming
Golf	Track and field
Horseback riding	Ventriloquism
Magic	Volleyball

If your child wants to paint, take the entire family out to a natural place so that your child can set up an easel and canvas while the other members of the family enjoy some fresh air nearby, occasionally checking on the progress of the painting and commenting on your child's technique or talent. If your child has found a particular genre or series of books to read avidly, set up a serene family reading hour, where all family members gather in a common room with their books and magazines, light a fire in the fireplace, and enjoy hot beverages and a plate of healthy snacks.

How you indulge your child's passions is up to you. As long as you convey to your child that investing energy in healthy activities can bring great rewards, and that they can enhance their enjoyment of activities if they simply stick with them, then you will have done a great thing.

Building on Their Passion

Once your child has selected a healthy activity or hobby that builds character, skill, or intellect, it is time to take advantage of his or her success. Use it as a launching point to encourage and build other important skills.

Finding a passion and pursuing it will help your child build confidence and self-worth, especially if that passion turns into a real talent. However, no one functions in our society with self-awareness alone; there are others with whom we all have to learn to interact, to work with, and to play with. Life is a team sport, and we have to get along with our teammates to play the game well.

If your child has developed a passion, then you already have a good starting point for setting up interactions with other kids. Nothing unites people more quickly than discovering that they have common interests. If your child enjoys reading, sign him or her up for book clubs at your local bookstore or public library. If your child has taken up an instrument, sign him or her up to play in an orchestra or encourage him or her to start a band. And, of course, if your child has developed new athleticism, have him or her try out for a sports team. Team sports will be discussed in greater detail in the following chapter on exercise—another integral part of the ADD/ADHD cure.

In less time than you might think, your child will be well on the way to reentering social circles and peer groups. Having an interest to share with others serves three very important functions: (1) it offers children a way to feel commonality and a community with others; (2) it effectively conveys to children that their worth is not determined by their weaknesses, but by their strengths and their own unique set of skills and talents; and (3) it imparts to them an awareness that everyone is very different and that they don't need to be ashamed of the ways in which they are different from others—ADD/ADHD or not.

8

Getting Your Kid to Get Up, Get Out, and Exercise!

You cannot get your child out the door to play soccer or basketball when you are sitting on the couch eating potato chips and watching television. Like all other aspects of this program, the changes you make regarding activity and exercise have to be family changes. You're all going to get more active, healthier, and happier . . . together. In addition to curing a case of ADD/ADHD, you'll also reap other health benefits.

Nine-year-old Oliver and his six-year-old brother, Victor, were two of my patients. Their parents, Ted and Jessica, had begun to suspect that their sons' wild behavior was not a product of shortcomings in their parenting skills. The boys were both diagnosed with ADD/ADHD. For a year before receiving the official diagnosis, Mom and Dad struggled to get the boys involved in team sports. First, they had Oliver signed up for club soccer, but within two months he had been kicked off the team for fighting with not only opposing team members but also his own teammates in both practice and during games. Their younger son, Victor, did no better in Little League baseball, where his parents noticed that he sat apart from the other kids in the dugout, and was eventually taken off the team after a scary episode in which he hurled his bat at the pitcher for striking him out. The boys both really had trouble with impulse control.

After the diagnosis, Ted and Jessica put their efforts to get their kids into team sports on hold. They even pulled their kids out of after-school activities because of problems with pushing and shoving and not following directions. The company that Jessica worked for allowed her to adjust her work schedule and do part of her work from home so she could administer her children's medication before school and keep them company after school. When the boys were home from school, Jessica found it easiest on her nerves and more practical for her work to let her sons spend the afternoon in front of the television with their favorite cartoons or video games.

Inactivity began to take its toll. Oliver and Victor were bored and tired by early evening. They grew unnaturally sleepy at around seven thirty. Between their sluggishness and the allure of the television, Jessica found it impossible to get them moving, let alone get them outside for sports. At first, she was concerned that her sons' fatigue was a side effect of the medication. When they both began to gain weight, however, she made the connection between their listlessness and their new sedentary lifestyle. She resolved to get the entire family healthy, and she and Ted gave me a call.

They were relieved to discover that their case was very common. Many children I see with ADD or ADHD have been banned from team sports or ostracized from after-school activities by their peers for being out of control. With few other obvious options for recreation, many of them resort to hours of watching television or playing video games to pass the time. Their parents, who are often exhausted from their jobs, child-care responsibilities, and other duties, are so grateful for the quiet time that they'll allow their children to waste hours of time this way.

I asked Jessica and Ted to begin the nutritional part of the boys' treatment first. The food at the after-school programs and the doughnuts and other junk food served after the kids' soccer and baseball games was bad enough. But at home, there was an even more relaxed attitude toward junk food, and chips, candy, and cookies were seemingly unlimited. A lot has been written about television watching creating obesity in American children, but it's really the high-calorie, greasy, sugary food combined with the television watching that's making our kids slow and fat. The family and I worked hard in making adjustments to their lifestyle. These involved turning off the television and putting on the athletic shoes. I asked the family to hike or play ball at least four or five days out of each week (preferably six or seven).

Ted, a busy insurance executive, resisted initially, arguing about how he needed the time to deal with paperwork from the office. Jessica resisted a little less, but she was concerned about the amount of housework that she needed to do. After lightly bickering over who had *less* time, they finally decided to commit to the new exercise program.

Combining a regular sugar-free diet and exercise, Oliver and Victor developed an entirely new and different attitude about family, school, and sports. The extreme ADD symptoms started to clear up within weeks. And within a few short months not only did the birthday party invitations start to come again, but the parents were also able to convince the soccer and Little League coaches to give their boys a second chance. Jessica and Ted were thrilled to see that their children could cooperate with their teammates while playing soccer and baseball.

The goal of this book is to either eliminate the need for ADD medication or to drastically reduce the dose of medication needed. The importance of exercise—as we strive to go medication free—cannot be stressed enough. Intuitively, we know that exercise makes us feel better and often "clears the mind." Countless medical researchers have verified this. Recent studies, such as the one designed and supervised by Dr. Michael S. Wendt at the State University of New York at Buffalo, revealed a marked improvement in the behavior of children with ADD and ADHD who began to exercise regularly. Dr. Wendt's study showed that increased respiratory rates cause increased oxygen intake, which leads to biochemical changes that promote healthy changes in brain chemistry. The subjects in Dr. Wendt's study showed significant improvements in behavior after only two to four weeks of regular moderate exercise done for forty minutes five days a week. These improvements came most dramatically in the area of oppositional behaviors, which are to blame for most conflicts that children with ADD and ADHD have with their peers, teachers, and family members.

These findings and the research conclusions of many other scientists confirm what doctors who care for ADD and ADHD patients already know. Diet combined with exercise works. But still, whenever I recommend family exercise as a way to control ADD and ADHD, I hear the same protests: "With my husband's work schedule, and my work/home schedule, and with the children's schoolwork, we don't have time to exercise as a family." I expect this resistance, I respectfully discuss it, and then I reject it as nicely as possible. For a child and family dealing with attention deficit issues, exercise cannot be regarded as an option. It is a crucial part of the cure. There is simply no substitute for its brain-changing benefits. I try not to be harsh when I tell parents, "I know that none of us thinks we have enough time for exercise, but we have to *make time.*" A great start would be to schedule exercise for at least half an hour for three to four days a week for the first few weeks. If we can project enthusiasm for exercise, then our children will become comfortable, if not wildly enthusiastic, about physical activity. The goal is to eventually move up to forty minutes to an hour of sustained physical activity five days a week (or ideally, every day), each and every week. The exercises need to have an aerobic element—something to get the heart rate up to 130–140 beats per minute. Baseball games are fun, but most of the time kids stand around in the outfield or sit on the bench. I'm talking about power walking, hiking, soccer, basketball—running-type activities that raise the heart and respiratory rate and increase fitness with every single outing. Even though these exercises can be combined with muscle-building/weight lifting, I prefer to focus on aerobic fitness.

For some parents, it takes an explanation of the technical reasons that exercise is necessary for them to finally be convinced. Expanding on what we learned through Dr. Wendt's study, I explain to them the following: that with sustained exercise, blood flow to the brain is increased. This stimulates the release of adrenaline, serotonin, and other important brain chemicals. Exercise also promotes the growth of neurons, or new brain cells, in the cerebellum and elsewhere. A brain that is constantly producing neurons is a brain that is operating at its peak and is much more resistant to negative chemical changes that adversely affect mood and prompt the difficult parts of ADD-type behavior. All parts of the brain benefit from exercise, from the highest lobes, which include the executive center of the brain, to the limbic system and the amygdala (emotional centers) and the cerebellum, which deals with coordination and balance. You can see that a child with ADD or ADHD can only benefit from the firing of neurons in all these areas. *Exercise* does this.

We've all heard that exercise releases endorphins into our bloodstream and that these brain chemicals make us feel good. Endorphins act as natural antidepressants and antianxiety agents.

A family-wide exercise program is often necessary because children trying to recover from ADD/ADHD are often still feeling the sting from being shunned by their classmates or former teammates. In addition to all the health benefits, playing sports together as a family can be viewed as training for children with ADD/ADHD so that they can eventually reintegrate into social groups or team settings with confidence and good sportsmanship. This training comes in the form of instilling a sense of structure into the children's lives—something that most kids with ADD/ADHD lack. In addition to being deprived of some self-regulating abilities because of ADD/ADHD, they often lack structure at home, where their behavior tends to make the household more chaotic.

These new family activities introduce the concepts of organization and cooperation into the children's lives. As children get better, these concepts can carry over into team sports, school activities, and birthday parties. You'll notice that I keep coming back to birthday parties. As I've mentioned before, it's one of the key subjects that I ask kids and parents about: How do you do at birthday parties? How much do you as parents look forward to birthday parties, and, by the way, have you noticed the number of invitations dropping?

You might not think that exercise could help fill your mailbox with birthday party invitations again, but it can.

Family Fun and Family Fitness

In choosing activities for your whole family, keep in mind the basic characteristics of a child with ADD/ADHD and your child's specific personality traits. These will help you understand your child's needs that can be successfully met through activity. Simply speaking, we all talk about the need to burn off excess energy. If your child has the hyperactivity type of ADD, healthy physical activity can serve as a safety valve so that this energy doesn't boil over or explode in more destructive and disruptive ways. Sometimes, the quickest and best ways to channel this energy are the simplest; you don't need special equipment or teammates for running, jogging, or hiking, and most communities have indoor pools where your child can swim year round.

Family Activities

Here are some activities you can do as a family to exercise and have fun together.

Running/Jogging/Biking

You don't even need to drive to a specific place. You can walk or run around your own neighborhood. Even in inclement weather, you can go outside if you have the right cold weather or rain gear. When the weather is nice, ride up and down the street on your bicycles, or pile into the car and take a trip to a local park or high school to run laps around a track. Set goals—personal and family—by using a stopwatch or a pedometer to time your runs.

Swimming

Swimming exercises all the major muscle groups at once, and this makes it the perfect activity for a child who wants to splash around, play games, or swim laps. Once a couple of laps have done the trick, the pool is a great place for games and some refreshing silliness. Marco Polo and underwater handstands are perennial favorites.

Sports

Unless you have a family of five to field a basketball team or eleven to field a soccer or football team, you may have trouble with some team sports. But the skills and sweat that go into those sports—kicking and passing a soccer ball, dribbling and passing a basketball, or practicing tennis strokes against a wall—can be done by families of two, three, or four. Practicing all these skills will make joining a team or reentering a team easier and more fun.

Activities to Keep Them Interested

Children with ADD/ADHD often have clever minds, and they may get bored more quickly than other children. Use your imagination to think of new activities and games to keep them interested. If you're having trouble, here are some suggestions.

Hiking

Camping or day trips to a nearby lake or river can be a lot easier than you think, and an occasional excursion to the great outdoors can be refreshing and renewing for any family, especially one that is dealing with ADD/ADHD. The scenery changes with every few steps, and you might even be tempted to go canoeing. Hiking, camping, and canoeing and kayaking sites are usually within an easy drive. And most families have nature trails integrated into some of the larger parks in their communities. You might even find an arboretum in the heart of the urban jungle. Do some research on the Internet, and you'll find great outdoor experiences.

Dancing

Enroll your family in a dance class or rent some instructional videos for your family to practice at home. Dance can encourage both lively physical activity and creativity in your child. Children love opportunities to act silly and to move freely. Dance offers your children the excuse to do just that.

Activities to Keep Them Challenged

With our guidance, children with ADD/ADHD can be moved toward athletic activities that challenge them physically and mentally. It's even better if there are definite goals and rewards for their efforts. Here are some recommended activities to keep your child challenged.

Building

Maybe this isn't exercise in the traditional sense, but a family construction project, whether it's building a doghouse or painting a room, can be a great diversion, educational opportunity, and physical challenge. The final product will serve as a constant and proud reminder of family accomplishment, teamwork, and cooperation.

Martial Arts

It's easy to enroll your family in martial arts lessons. The great benefits of having children with ADD/ADHD train in kung fu, tae kwon do, or karate is that, for the most part, their biggest challenger will be themselves. Many martial arts classes use a degree system that is represented with colored belts that students can earn as they push themselves to improve. Additionally, all martial arts promote a high level of self-discipline, something that most children with ADD and ADHD naturally lack. Although the lessons may involve some sparring with other students and therefore may raise parents' concerns about aggression, any physical contact between students is closely monitored by a mentor, who often also serves as a positive role model and authority figure whom kids can look up to. And if you're still concerned about physical contact, there are plenty of classes that require that students perform their moves only on punching bags or while standing in place. As for the parents, most martial arts studios have great classes for adult beginners. They'll make it fun while making sure you don't get a bloody nose, and the entire family can progress from the white belt to the yellow belt together. Families that take classes together can also practice together at home—in the living room, in the backyard, or at the local park—and support and congratulate one another through advancements from one belt to the next.

Getting Your Child Invited Back to the Team

When all the adjustments in diet and regular family exercise have worked their magic and your child is well on his or her way to leading a childhood free of drugs and ADD/ADHD symptoms, let's get them invited back to the soccer, baseball, or basketball team.

Exercising as a family has already taught your child the crucial social skills they lacked when they tried to participate in team sports before. You've used and have continued to use this active time together to demonstrate and compliment good sportsmanship. Your child has learned self-discipline, graceful losing, *and* gracious winning. And the key to all of this has been cooperation. The whole family has cooperated and encouraged one another. It's time to put these skills to work on a team. It might feel tricky or even difficult to get your child to rejoin a team (whether a sports team, a band, or a drama group) because of previous bad experiences, but as I've said, the kids who are the most reluctant about these activities are the ones who benefit from and need them the most. Mom and Dad and the whole family have spent hours learning skills that apply everywhere—at school, in group projects, at parties, and in work settings.

You can see how the value of regular exercise and physical interaction with family and friends is immeasurable in the long run for someone who struggles with ADD/ADHD. Your family can use the following chart to determine the best exercises for your child, based on their main benefits, and to create a structured exercise program that accompanies the diet program for the full thirty days of the ADD and ADHD cure. A structured exercise program will help your family become acclimated to the idea and practice of making fitness a daily priority.

EXERCISE BENEFITS

	Very Aerobic	Allows for Creativity/ Improvising	Satisfies a Need for Novelty	Presents Mental Challenges	Builds Coordination	Teaches Social Skills	Can Be Clearly Measured
Running/ jogging	✔						✔
Swimming	✔	✔			✔		
Biking	✔				✔		✔
Hiking		✔	✔	✔	✔	✔	✔
Canoeing/ kayaking	✔		✔		✔	✔	✔
Martial arts		✔	✔	✔	✔		✔
Dancing		✔	✔		✔		
Basketball	✔				✔	✔	
Soccer	✔				✔	✔	
Tennis	✔				✔	✔	
Baseball/ softball					✔	✔	
Football	✔				✔	✔	
Volleyball					✔	✔	
Table tennis	✔				✔	✔	
Badminton					✔	✔	
Construction projects		✔	✔	✔		✔	✔

The ADD/ ADHD Cure Thirty-Day Exercise Program

The following program is designed to get your whole family moving again—at first, for most days of the week, and then every day. Each day's program is structured to provide your child with clear time limits and goals, and involves a variety of activities in each aerobic session to hold his or her attention.

If you and your family do the exercises with your child, it will be a fun group activity and will foster support, cooperation, and togetherness. Using a stopwatch is a great idea because it helps to enforce the structure of each exercise session and it marks the end of a task, which comes with a feeling of accomplishment, especially if you all remember to congratulate one another after each activity for a job well done.

Remember to always warm up before beginning any exercise routine, to encourage your child to *keep moving* even when it starts to feel difficult, and to stay hydrated with water throughout the routine and afterward.

Week 1

Monday

- 5 minutes of warming up and jogging
- 10 minutes of an aerobic activity (running, swimming laps, biking, jumping rope, doing jumping jacks, etc.)
- 10 minutes of a different aerobic activity
- 5 minutes of free aerobic play (dancing to music, imitating animals, playing "follow the leader," etc.)
- Total time: 30 minutes

Tuesday

- Rest
  - It's important on "rest" days to involve your child in planning the exercises that the family will do together the next day and getting him or her excited about it. This creates the impression from the

very first week that exercise is something to look forward to, not something to be dreaded as a chore.

Wednesday

- 5 minutes of warming up and jogging
- 10 minutes of an aerobic activity
- 10 minutes of a different aerobic activity
- 5 minutes of free aerobic play
- Total time: 30 minutes

Thursday

- Rest

Friday

- 5 minutes of stretching and jogging
- 10 minutes of an aerobic activity
- 10 minutes of a different aerobic activity
- 5 minutes of free aerobic play
- Total time: 30 minutes

Saturday

- Rest

Sunday

- Family sport day
  - Find a sport your whole family can do together: one-on-one or two-on-two basketball, tennis, volleyball, tetherball, touch football, and Ping-Pong are good options.
  - Remember to keep the energy level high and the pace quick so it can get as close to an aerobic activity as possible.
- Total time: Up to one hour

Week 2

Monday

- 5 minutes of warming up and jogging
- 10 minutes of an aerobic activity
- 10 minutes of a different aerobic activity
- 10 minutes of a different aerobic activity
- 5 minutes of free aerobic play
- Total time: 40 minutes

Tuesday

- Rest

Wednesday

- 5 minutes of warming up and jogging
- 10 minutes of an aerobic activity
- 10 minutes of a different aerobic activity
- 10 minutes of a different aerobic activity
- 5 minutes of free aerobic play
- Total time: 40 minutes

Thursday

- Rest

Friday

- 5 minutes of warming up and jogging
- 10 minutes of an aerobic activity
- 10 minutes of a different aerobic activity
- 10 minutes of a different aerobic activity
- 5 minutes of free aerobic play
- Total time: 40 minutes

Saturday

- Free play day
  - Designate an hour during the day when your child has to do something active. Make sure he or she keeps moving, or better yet, actively participate. It can be biking around the neighborhood, playing tag in the yard, or even swimming in the community pool. Let your child choose the activity, and it will end up being more fun for everyone.
  - If your child has difficulty self-motivating, let him or her pick a dance or martial arts class to go to once or twice a week, to substitute for the free play day.
- Total time: Up to one hour

Sunday

- Family sport day
- Total time: Up to one hour

Week 3

Monday

- 5 minutes of warming up and jogging
- 10 minutes of an aerobic activity
- 10 minutes of a different aerobic activity
- 10 minutes of a different aerobic activity
- 5 minutes of free aerobic play
- Total time: 40 minutes

Tuesday

- Free play day
- Total time: Up to one hour

Wednesday

- 5 minutes of warming up and jogging
- 10 minutes of an aerobic activity
- 10 minutes of a different aerobic activity
- 10 minutes of a different aerobic activity
- 5 minutes of free aerobic play
- Total time: 40 minutes

Thursday

- Rest

Friday

- 5 minutes of warming up and jogging
- 10 minutes of an aerobic activity
- 10 minutes of a different aerobic activity
- 10 minutes of a different aerobic activity
- 5 minutes of free aerobic play
- Total time: 40 minutes

Saturday

- Free play day
- Total time: Up to one hour

Sunday

- Family sport day
- Total time: Up to one hour

Week 4

Monday

- 5 minutes of warming up and jogging
- 10 minutes of an aerobic activity
- 10 minutes of a different aerobic activity
- 10 minutes of a different aerobic activity
- 5 minutes of free aerobic play
- Total time: 40 minutes

Tuesday

- Free play day
- Total time: Up to one hour

Wednesday

- 5 minutes of warming up and jogging
- 10 minutes of an aerobic activity
- 10 minutes of a different aerobic activity
- 10 minutes of a different aerobic activity
- 5 minutes of free aerobic play
- Total time: 40 minutes

Thursday

- Family sport day
- Total time: Up to one hour

Friday

- 5 minutes of warming up and jogging
- 10 minutes of an aerobic activity

- 10 minutes of a different aerobic activity
- 10 minutes of a different aerobic activity
- 5 minutes of free aerobic play
- Total time: 40 minutes

Saturday

- Free play day
- Total time: Up to one hour

Sunday

- Family sport day
- Total time: Up to one hour

PART III

The Home Stretch, and Beyond

9

Doing More: Additional Natural Treatments

Total Wellness, and Then Some

By now, you understand that proper nutrition can alleviate the most troubling symptoms of ADD/ADHD, and it might get rid of them altogether. If you've already begun the thirty-day treatment plan, then you're enjoying the tremendous benefits that good food and an active lifestyle bring, not only to one who suffers from ADD/ADHD but to anyone who has made the effort to eat better and live better.

You know, as I wrote the words "thirty-day treatment plan," it looked like a short time to me. I hope it doesn't feel like a long time to you. Thirty days of eating great, exercising, and getting enough sleep, compared to three, four, or fifteen years of medication, sounds like a wonderful prospect to me. Improved health comes easier than you once thought, and with wellness comes the clarity to be productive in work and the energy to enjoy playtime to the fullest.

The diet and exercise regimen are at the core of the cure, but I'd like to offer you some additional treatments to reinforce your child's and your family's health. Quite frankly, I learned nothing in medical school about the natural path to stress relief, anxiety relief, and improvement in concentration. Even my medical school professors couldn't possibly argue with things as gentle and beneficial as yoga for a five-year-old, safe herbal therapy for a seven-year-old, or acupuncture for a ten-year-old. The Western medical community has ended the debate over whether Eastern medicine and holistic therapies are effective, and the answer is yes. A few years ago, the *Journal of American Medical Association* devoted an entire issue to complementary medicine. It talked about herbal treatment, acupuncture, and more. In the past ten years, there have been thousands of research papers in conventional medical journals on these topics. Alternative treatments share the common characteristic of maximum effect with minimal side effects. There have been a number of studies (including peer-reviewed research conducted by the National Institute of Mental Health) showing that treatments that combine traditional ADD/ADHD medicines with complementary treatments are more effective than the medication alone.

Alternative treatments may not help in every case, but they can be used safely. Consult your physician before changing the doses of your child's medication, and don't be discouraged if your doctor reluctantly approves but doesn't enthusiastically endorse these methods. Still, despite the minimal risk attached to most natural therapies, you may feel more confident if you talk to your child's physician first. I still encourage you to do your own research and exercise your own good judgment. Unfortunately, most doctors are far too skeptical about complementary medicine.

If you give yourself the go-ahead regarding complementary medicine, you just might discover that it can be fun and inspiring to look for and find natural treatments for your child and family. Finding a natural treatment that works—to use in addition to good nutrition and exercise—amounts to an exciting discovery for everyone involved. Nobody knows your child better than you do, and taking more control over his or her health empowers you and your child. For those families interested in complementary therapies, I am happy to suggest yoga, acupuncture, herbal medicines, and dietary supplements.

Trying natural treatments takes patience. In fact, the main reason the medical community has a difficult time studying alternative treatments is because the results vary from individual to individual, and none of the treatments can offer any guarantees. However, you should know that they differ in their effects because they work *with* a person's body, and everybody is different.

A simplification that I use when discussing conventional versus complementary medicine is that conventional medicine tends to work against the body's natural, often beneficial functioning. For example, if you have a fever and take an aspirin, the fever goes away, even though that fever may shorten the duration of an infection. If you have a stuffy nose and take a decongestant, the stuffy nose goes away, even though that stuffiness comes from blood vessels dilated to deliver more white blood cells to an infected area. Complementary medicine usually works much more slowly and gradually with the body's normal physiology. Again, this is a simplification, but it's a pretty accurate one.

Mind and Body

Families that deal with ADD/ADHD know very well that the mind and the body are closely linked. Even a small junk-food binge can send our children right over the edge. An ADD/ADHD drug that supposedly helps to control anxiety and improve concentration might temporarily slow growth, interfere with good sleep, and lead to difficult behavior later in the day as the medication wears off. Conversely, properly caring for the body with good nutrition and exercise yields the reward of *natural* mental and emotional stability. For families dealing with ADD or ADHD, the mind-body link is not some loopy, New Age concept—it's something that needs to be monitored on a daily basis.

A lot of natural treatments you'll find today have a focus in strengthening the connection between the mind and the body, or relaxing the mind and the body so that a person can more easily bring himself or herself to mental clarity and focus. These relaxed states combat hyperactivity, anxiety, and depression. More than that, they are often fun and interesting to try, and the sessions take place in controlled settings and environments where children with ADD/ADHD will be less prone to act up or out. Tens of thousands of people—from corporate executives to college kids, teenagers, and, increasingly, small children—are becoming enthusiastic participators in mind-body relaxation routines like yoga classes and acupuncture.

I don't claim to have received any formal training in complementary or alternative medicine, but in my practice I have seen enough success with it that I readily recommend it to all my patients.

Yoga

Yoga originated in India more than three thousand years ago and is now incredibly popular in our modern world as a way to improve the health of both mind and body. It is a controlled fusion of breathing techniques, postures and stretches, meditation, and relaxation. Many people who once found themselves stressed out by their jobs or home lives now swear by the stress-relieving, anxiety-reducing benefits of yoga. It is known to improve one's feelings of well-being and bring whipped-up emotions into a state of calm and quiet. One recent study involving adults who practiced yoga revealed that many experienced a measurable drop in anger, tension, and hyperactivity. The study also showed that those who participated in yoga more intensely and at greater frequency (adding home practice to their time in a yoga studio or at a gym) experienced an even greater dip in these symptoms. In other words, there was a clear connection between the amount of yoga practiced and the amount of emotional well-being experienced.

The effectiveness of yoga in bringing these benefits can be traced to its focus on deep breathing and on opening up the body for better breath intake. During these exercises, the heart rate is reduced as the body relaxes and the breathing becomes slow and steady. Learning to slow one's breathing and to simply relax in times of high anxiety is perhaps the greatest skill yoga offers those who struggle with ADD or ADHD. Higher levels of oxygen delivered to the brain produce greater concentration and alertness in everyone, not just people who have difficulty focusing.

Yoga is such a mainstream practice that most health clubs and gyms offer yoga classes as part of their regular schedules. Adults in our society certainly need them; workplace pressures and the demands of raising families can get stifling, and without healthy outlets to alleviate stress, many of us would be tearing our hair out at the roots. Pressure is an inescapable part of work and home life for adults. Homework, the classroom dynamic, and social pressures are things that typically introduce a lot of stress into the lives of school-age children. As a result, many yoga studios now offer classes for kids. Some elementary schools have also begun offering yoga, inviting special instructors to come to the school to lead sessions. With a little research, you'll surely find access to a place where your entire family can enjoy yoga at a location near you.

Meditation and Tai Chi

In addition to yoga, there are several other exercises and practices you can find that will help to bring the body to relaxation, primarily through breathing. These include traditional meditation and the Chinese martial art of tai chi.

Simply put, meditation is training your mind to relax so that it can focus on other things afterward. Many self-help books and business books recommend meditation to reduce stress and to prepare the mind for challenging tasks that might bring stress. The type of meditation your family can learn (even as part of a yoga class) will have its focus on helping you and your child loosen up, mellow out, and calm down.

If you find a class or a program that will teach you and your child to meditate, you'll be instructed to move your body in postures designed to open up your lungs and stretch and relax your muscles. Your instructor might ask you to envision certain images in your mind, with the objective of stopping the mind from racing or wandering so you can concentrate on controlled breathing. It will be difficult at first for your child to hold onto a solid meditative state because children with ADD/ADHD have minds that work overtime. However, keeping with a program of meditation makes it easier and easier. You'll eventually see that when your child is able to summon up calm at will just by going through meditative motions, the symptoms of ADD/ADHD can naturally melt away whenever he or she needs them to in times of stress and frustration.

Tai chi is another meditative art, and although there is a martial form of it that can be used in hand-to-hand combat, the form of it that will benefit your child is the one you'll often see groups of elderly Chinese men and women doing in a park. It is a centuries-old East Asian art with a focus on controlled, slow-motion kung-fu movements (unlike yoga and traditional meditation, which utilize poses and postures) and regulated breathing. It is useful in diminishing anxiety and depression, and millions of Chinese are believers in its benefits. If you can find an instructor in your area (I would recommend checking martial arts studios), it promises to be an interesting way to rein in stress and anxiety. Plus, if your child expresses any interest in incorporating a martial art like kung fu, aikido, or tae kwon do into his or her exercise regimen, tai chi can be a good gateway activity or a complementary one.

Acupuncture

Acupuncture has ancient origins but has now fully entered into mainstream practice. You'll find acupuncture clinics in most cities, which are owned by practitioners who are educated in accredited alternative medicine colleges and universities that are licensed by the state. Major universities, including the University of California at Los Angeles, have prestigious schools and research centers dedicated to studying alternative and complementary medicine and to training medical students in these practices. The benefits of acupuncture have been so established that more and more health insurance providers are including acupuncture among the tretments that they cover.

You may have already seen acupuncture in practice or, given its prevalence, tried it yourself at some point. It involves the insertion of very fine needles into specific points on the body. The needles are so thin that they produce no more than a small prick when inserted, and the site of insertion does not produce blood when the needle is removed. The points where they are inserted fall along meridians that have been mapped out by traditional Chinese medical practitioners through trial and error over thousands of years. These meridians and the medical science behind them are widely studied in Europe and the United States.

Through acupuncture we learn that certain points on our body match up to the control and function of different muscles and organs. The stimulation of the nerves in these points with needles can restore "balance" to a body by improving the function of certain systems and/or by alleviating pain that is exacerbating an illness or condition.

Often, acupuncture is used for pain management following a muscle injury or is used to induce relaxation in people who suffer from great stress. The benefits of acupuncture vary, and acupuncturists design treatments to meet the needs of their patients. Many adults with ADD/ADHD who have discovered acupuncture typically use it to alleviate the troublesome side effects that come from taking their medication, such as dizziness, fatigue, sleeplessness, and abdominal pain. As interest and confidence in pediatric acupuncture has grown, this use of the treatment has been extended to children.

Apart from relief from side effects, unmedicated children and teens can discover many more beneficial uses of acupuncture, as long as the needles don't frighten them in the first session (because the needles often don't hurt when they are inserted, I know of many children who find the sight of the needles in their skin kind of funny.) When your child goes in for a session, there are many approaches that an acupuncturist may take with him or her. There are some points that alleviate stress. Some points boost immune system function, some improve concentration, some energize the body, and some regulate sleep. An acupuncturist will tailor your child's treatment to the most persistent of his or her symptoms.

After the needles are inserted, the patient will lie still for some time, breathing steadily as the needles are allowed to do their work, with occasional adjustment from the doctor. Having needles in one's body is a good enough reason for most of us to lie still, and in children with ADD/ADHD, it encourages them to learn how to be comfortable with calmly lying still.

Because acupuncture can be a little alarming to look at for young children, I recommend that you receive treatment alongside your child when going in for the first time. If it doesn't work well enough for either of you, it will at least be an interesting shared experience, and both of you will forever be able to say, "Been there! Done that!"

Herbal Remedies

My expertise in herbal medicine is limited, and so I tend to play it safe and recommend simple herbal remedies for my patients. When it comes to alleviating ADD/ADHD symptoms, I frequently suggest the following herbs.

- *Aspalathus linearis* (rooibos): improves nutrient absorption, alleviates insomnia, is rich in antioxidants

- *Avena sativa* (oat straw): balances blood-sugar levels, promotes health of the nervous and hormonal systems, alleviates mild depression, exhaustion, and insomnia

- *Ginkgo biloba*: enhances concentration, increases cerebral blood flow, alleviates anxiety and depression, promotes health in the brain and the central nervous system, is rich in antioxidants

- *Matricaria recutita* (German chamomile, or simply, chamomile): helps relieve anxiety, alleviates insomnia, has many antioxidant properties

- *Melissa officinalis* (lemon balm): relieves depression, improves mood, balances hormones

Beyond this, I recommend that you find a specialist in herbal medicine to individualize a treatment plan for your child. Please remember that even though herbal medicines are natural, they can have very strong effects, and when taken in incorrect amounts can produce undesired effects. You'll want an expert to guide your decisions if you're going to experiment with herbal treatments beyond the basic ones listed here.

Natural, drug-free symptom relief is a boon, and finding something that treats ADD or ADHD symptoms that is both fun and relaxing is a cause for celebration. Do not be discouraged if any of these treatments do not bring immediate positive results for your child; trying them out together should be treated as an adventure.

Remember that no matter how effective one of these treatments might be for your child, a healthy diet and an active lifestyle remain at the core of the cure. All other therapies should be treated as complements to the main treatment, like appetizers and side dishes to a healthy main course.

10

Revisiting School Choices

Having achieved an internal balance within your family, it's time to consider school choices. Your child's future is looking bright, and so those bad impressions and negative relationships left over from his or her past may only be holding him or her back. Rethinking your child's school choices may help him or her realize his or her full potential in the future.

When and if you decide that your child's current educational environment isn't the optimal one, you'll need to weigh anew all of your child's educational options on their merits. You must begin to think in terms of an education program that is geared toward building on the hard-won gains your child has been making since you adopted the ADD and ADHD cure. In the right environment, your child can continue to make progress toward realizing his or her full potential. Needless to say, your next decision is important.

How to Choose a School

Gather information by talking to other parents, visiting a few schools, and realizing that there probably isn't one "right" choice. Your best information will be gathered from school visits and conversations with teachers and school administrators about their feelings regarding learning differences. You don't need to present the hardest aspects of your child's behaviors. However, you do need to get an idea of how teachers and administrators feel about the uniqueness in each child.

I've spoken to hundreds of parents who visited dozens of schools and had dozens of conversations with teachers and administrators and still agonized over the decision of where to send their child. The decision is not irrevocable. You can exert a strong influence on your child's behavior and development, and if things aren't going well, your child can change schools. Here are some things to consider when choosing a school.

- Is the class size small enough so that your child will get plenty of attention?
- Does the school look safe and secure to you?
- Do the teachers and school administrators have experience taking care of a diverse group of kids, including kids with ADD/ADHD?

When to Change Schools

No matter how carefully you choose a school, sometimes it just doesn't work out. Before you consider a change in school, talk to the teachers and administrators to see if they can shed light on why your child is not having a good experience and what can be done about it. Talk to your child about the problems he or she is having without casting blame on the teachers or other kids; and certainly do not judge your child. Give the school time to solve the problems your child is having. Any child, with or without ADD/ADHD needs time to adjust, and frequent school changes are not good for anybody.

But if the school is unwilling or unable to work with your child, then it's time to look for a new school. When choosing a new school, try not to pick one that is a great distance from your house. If your child has to get up extremely early and/or has a long commute to school, it may be hard for him or her to attend playdates and birthday parties and participate in outdoor activities after school.

Overall, set aside your preconceived notions about the best academic setting in favor of realizing that your child's uniqueness needs to be matched with the best school for him or her. There are schools specifically created to take care of the needs of ADD/ADHD children. They're found mostly in big cities, but even in smaller cities or towns you can find schools that have classes and programs created to meet your child's specific needs. Also look into after-school programs like social skills classes that address the challenges for children with impulse control and attention issues.

The following lists outline some of the benefits and drawbacks of both traditional and homeschooling. My biggest reservation about homeschooling is the same as my reservation about kids not joining soccer, basketball, or other sports teams. Children who pull away from and don't do well in groups, whether it's teams or classes, are the ones who probably will benefit the most from these situations.

Traditional Schooling vs. Homeschooling

STAYING IN CURRENT SCHOOL

Pros

- Less traumatic.
- Allows continuity of friendships already made.

Cons

- The relationships a child has formed with teachers and peers may make change difficult.
- These same relationships may impede or reverse the progress that you've made with the family at home.
- Discouragement from teachers and peers may impede the progress that you've made at home.

CHANGING SCHOOL

Pros

- The child gets a fresh start—with teachers, with friends, and with his or her feelings about himself or herself.

Cons

- Can be socially disruptive for the child.

- The child may blame himself or herself.

- A new setting may be stressful to adjust to and can bring about a relapse in ADD/ADHD symptoms.

- The child may have to struggle to catch up with academic materials and to fit into established groups of friends.

HOMESCHOOLING

Pros

- You can customize a lesson plan to your child's specific educational level, and move at the pace that is most manageable for him or her.

- Your child can learn in an environment filled with your values and beliefs.

- There will be fewer negative messages for your child about his or her particular learning differences.

Cons

- The child loses the valuable experience of being at school and managing social pressures.

- The child misses out on certain opportunities to make friends and may find it more difficult to adjust and form friendships if he or she returns to regular schooling.

- You need to make certain that your curriculum matches the one used in school.

In some cases, especially those involving private schools, you may be encouraged by the administrators at your child's educational institution to keep your child where he or she is. They may try to convince you of the risk of trauma to your child, and they may tell you that the same problems your child encounters there will crop up again at other schools. Even though the pluses and minuses of a child's history can travel from the old school to the new one, a fresh start may still make the most sense. Schools that counsel parents not to withdraw their child may be influenced by the desire to keep the child's place in the class filled. Or they may feel that they're in the best position to help your child, or that your child's problem needs to be resolved with medication, no matter where he or she goes for schooling. Remember that it's your decision, and that other people have their own motivations for trying to sway your decisions that may not be in your best interest or in the best interest of your child. No one is in a better position to assess your child's position than you are, but by now, you know that.

Private School versus Public School

Private schools can be expensive and even out of reach financially for many families. Also note that private schools can accept, reject, or eject your child for a variety of reasons. However, if you find a private school that is the right match for your child but is unaffordable, you can explore two options: (1) many private schools have scholarship programs (2) with the proper advocacy and investigation, you may discover that your public school system is legally obligated to fund the right educational experience—including private school—for your child with ADD/ADHD.

The public school system will argue that it has programs in place for children with special needs. My experience is that even though these programs work for some kids with ADD/ADHD, they fail to meet the needs of other children. Please don't be discouraged or deterred by the initial denials of your requests to the public school system. Persistence will show that you're serious and that your child's educational rights need to be taken very seriously as well.

When to *Not* Change Schools

Let the school help you make this decision, but know that it's not the school's decision, it's yours. Talk to your child, but it certainly isn't his or her decision, either. The decision has to be based on what you feel is best for your child, realizing that change can be expensive, inconvenient, disruptive, and even traumatic for your child and for you.

I believe that allowing children to overcome social and educational challenges is so good for them that the default option is to stay at the same school. I think this is true even if your child protests. Get the teacher's opinions about what's going on with your child. If necessary, ask that a psychologist or an educational therapist observe your child in class. Then you, your child's teacher, and the expert can discuss these professional observations and make adjustments before a change in schools is considered.

There exists no ideal educational environment for your child. All teachers try to share their time and attention appropriately with each child in the classroom, accepting that some children may require more. This usually does not escape the notice of other kids in class. It's a rare class, and a rarer school, that's free of intolerant children. Children of all ages can be mean to one another, so no matter where your child receives his or her education, he or she needs to learn how to be self-sufficient in dealing with others. Slowly but surely, your child needs to learn how to be self-sufficient in completing assignments with less supervision. Learning how to cooperate with peers in a class or play situation will be more difficult for children with ADD/ADHD, and the best teachers know this. The ADD and ADHD cure helps a child improve his or her mental function and reduce the swings in mood and attention that poor nutrition can bring about, but it may not eliminate them. Your child's personal challenges may be carried from school to school, so I don't always immediately accept school changes as the best choice, and I don't take school changes lightly. Even with the best of intentions, your child's life and social development may be adversely affected as he or she goes from the familiar, as bad as it might be, to a new situation. Be aware of how vulnerable a child is during this time.

Your child doesn't have to be happy and eager about making a new life in a new school. But if your child is terrified about the idea of changing schools, you need to understand why and weigh the benefits of staying with a school against the benefits of leaving.

Established friendships at the old school are not to be discounted. If your child has formed a strong bond with friends or a teacher, it is an indication that he or she is *capable* of healthy, normal relationships. Ask yourself how much his or her sense of self-worth would be adversely affected if he or she leaves behind these relationships by going to a new school. If you decide that a school change is *still* the best option, you can help your child join you in this choice by couching the topic in a very positive way with the following questions:

- Isn't it exciting that in your new class there will be new friends and probably someone you know from your soccer team/your dance class?

- Would you like to see if you'll be happier in a new environment?

- Before you go to a new school, would you like it if we all went there to meet the teacher?

- If you started over at a new school, do you think it might be easier to do your schoolwork?

Speak with all the relevant people about this change: teachers, your pediatrician, parents and students at the new school, and your child's therapist or psychologist. Your intent is to be clear about your reasons and your perceived need for change. Make it very clear that this is not a whimsical decision and that you appreciate everybody's help and support.

Regardless of the changes you choose to make, keep in mind that human beings are highly adaptable. There is no purely right or wrong choice, but it is crucial that you monitor your child closely following *any* change, and be brave enough to move forward with further changes or even to revert back to a previous state as your situation evolves and calls for it.

11

Support for the Whole Family

ADD and ADD-type behavior are worsened or even brought on by bad nutrition, lack of exercise, lack of sleep, and lack of structure. You've looked at this book or maybe even have read it from cover to cover, and everything has started to improve because you used your common sense, love, and creativity to change your lifestyle for your child and family. Having a child with ADD or ADHD may be hard for every member of the family, and you may have had to repair relationships that were weakened by the stress of behavioral challenges.

You've put it all behind you. You're moving forward. You're eating differently. You're running together. You've learned new ways of relating to one another as a family.

Everyone in the family has learned to be respectful of the particular nutritional needs of the child with ADD/ADHD. Everybody in the family has gotten healthier because of the nutritional changes and increased physical activity. I'm not trying to pretend that all of this hasn't been annoying to the big sister, little brother, or maybe even the parents themselves. I'm not trying to pretend that your child with ADD/ADHD was thrilled when you replaced his sugar-frosted junk cereal with oatmeal, pancakes, or a tofu scramble. You may need to keep talking to one another about all of these changes because backsliding can be tempting for all members of the family. Please don't let it happen. You'll have to be especially strong on special occasions such as birthday parties, weddings, and Halloween parties. And while I may recommend near perfection, there will be some days where you may have to accept the regression and behavior brought on by "celebration food."

Sibling Support

The siblings of a child with ADD/ADHD might be concerned about or helpful to a brother or a sister with the disorder, but just as often, they can't believe that they have to go through the inconvenience of schedule and meal changes. They may not understand why they have to deal with this. They might actually be really embarrassed by their ADD/ADHD sibling's behavior at school and in social situations, or they may nobly try to defend their sibling and get ridiculed as a result. They might not want to discuss their feelings with you because they feel guilty that they even have these feelings. But you have to talk to them and get them to keep talking.

An added problem for siblings is that they may feel shortchanged, and maybe even *be* shortchanged, at home. Their brother or sister with ADD/ADHD is taking a lot of their parents' time and energy. This can entail dealing with behavioral disruption or missing fun events because the ADD/ADHD sibling can't attend. They may even face scolding or punishment for not dealing with the situation the way you want them to deal with it. In some cases, the family finances may have been diverted to tutors and other help for the ADD/ADHD child, and the siblings may have to forego some needed or wanted item. They might even misinterpret all the extra time and attention that the ADD/ADHD sibling is getting as a privilege, and they may feel that their sibling is getting more *love*.

I can think of many families where a sibling became an at-risk child because of the family stress dealing with ADD/ADHD. The feelings can arise from feeling deprived, but I've actually seen this created by the empathy that the sibling had for his or her sister or brother with ADD/ADHD. I like to remember Melissa, the older sister of James—a seven-year-old boy who had a severe case of ADHD. Melissa was nine and very mature for her age. She was well aware of her own extraordinary maturity, although her parents weren't. In fact, she seemed to think her parents weren't aware of many things.

I was surprised one day when I was told by the receptionist at my office that I had "a Melissa" waiting on the phone line for me. As I went into my office to take the call, I racked my brains for a patient or a parent I might have been treating at the time named Melissa, and I was drawing a blank. As it turned out, this was because Melissa wasn't a patient, although she had plenty of emotional issues she needed help with, and she was bright enough to recognize this herself.

A visit from the whole family was scheduled to take place later that week, and Melissa had snuck into her room with the phone to secretly call my office beforehand. She wanted to bring up her concerns with me in hopes that I would discuss these issues when her family came in. She thought her parents would never listen to her if *she* complained and that it would take another adult to bring up her concerns for them to listen. That she felt so ignored and undervalued that she had to sneak away to contact me without her parents' knowledge was really very striking. It sent a clear message to me that she felt neglected. Her parents, who were doing the best they could with the child who needed more care, were unaware that she felt this way. Melissa and I spoke on the phone for twenty minutes, and she sure did have a lot of complaints. She never or rarely spoke up about her negative feelings, and now that she had the opportunity to let it all out, she had a lot to say. She told me about the time she ate all her food at dinner while her brother pushed most of his food off his plate with the fork. When he finally put a piece of broccoli in his mouth, his parents praised him endlessly and told him he was a "good boy," while Melissa had sat there in front of her own plate, which she had cleaned, without receiving any praise. When she got up to put her dish in the sink, her father snapped at her for not excusing herself from the table first. She complained about a low test score on a spelling test she received because her parents were too busy to help her study. She complained that she had to hold her brother's hand in public places, and how she was yelled at if she let go of it even for just a second to scratch her nose. The list of complaints and of episodes that had upset her seemed to go on endlessly.

Melissa was very smart in asking for help, because she was absolutely right. In her family's case, her parents needed to hear it from someone on the outside, especially because they had gotten in the habit of devoting most of their attention to their other child. Later in my office, I asked her parents outright whether they felt they paid enough attention to Melissa. "Lucky for us, she doesn't need that much attention," her mom said with pride. She patted a sheepish-looking Melissa's head. "Melissa takes care of herself." There was obviously much misunderstanding and a failure to communicate in this family. I asked Melissa if she agreed completely, and if there were areas in which she felt she'd like more help or attention. Embarrassed now that she was on the spot, Melissa offered an abridged and less emotionally charged version of the complaints she had shared with me earlier that week on the phone.

In private later, I told Melissa and James's parents that Melissa was craving attention, and her own sacrifices and admirable responsibility were going unnoticed and unrewarded. I showed them how they could tell Melissa what an important part of the team she was if they only made a few adjustments in their version of the ADD and ADHD cure. The following were my suggestions to them to foster a sense of unity and support all around. These suggestions can apply to any version of the cure that involves siblings.

- If siblings are older than the child with ADD/ADHD, get them to take part in the planning of the daily meals, playtime hours, and so forth. If their opinions are taken into account, they'll feel more like willing participants in the plan rather than people upon whom the plan is forced, for no reasons that apply directly to them.

- Try your best to be more balanced in your awarding of praise. If your child with ADD/ADHD is doing something correctly, notice and thank the siblings for setting fine examples with their own appropriate behavior.

- Any special tutors or caretakers you hire should be informed that if the siblings have questions about their homework or need assistance with their tasks, they should try to extend their help to them as well. You should assure the siblings that anyone brought into the home to "help out" is there to help everyone.

- Older siblings can't be expected to act like responsible adults. Try to understand their motivations when they seem to act out, and ask yourself if you can lessen the resentment that they are feeling.

- Younger siblings might be a little harder to work with. They may not understand exactly what's going on, and perhaps one of the best things you can do for them is to treat them to a special outing apart from the child with ADD/ADHD every once in a while. Thank them for their patience and give them lots of opportunities to express themselves. Let them know you appreciate their cooperation as the family makes its changes.

Parental Guidance (Guidance for Parents!)

When I go to the hospital to examine a newborn, after I've discussed the baby's anatomy, I make certain to open a discussion of the new family dynamics. The first thing I say to the parents is: *Take good care of yourselves*. Each of your children, if they're smart (and they are!), will try to get 100 percent of your time and energy. If you do that math, you'll see that this just doesn't work. Take a little time each day for deep breaths and some time to be together as *a couple*. As I write this, I hope that you don't think that I think this is always easy. Accept the offer of friends who want to take one child to the park while you devote extra time and energy to your other child. And while you're at it, accept the offer of family and friends who want to take *all* the children to the park while you get a day or a night off. This advice applies to all couples, but may be even more important for families with an ADD/ADHD child.

Couples

A frequent complaint I hear from couples with children—not just those struggling with ADD or ADHD—is that the marriage took a dive once the first child was born. First to go is the romance, as both mother and father rearrange their priorities to put the welfare of the child above their own and that of their significant other. In the case of a child with ADD or ADHD, the amount of time and attention devoted to child rearing increases as the child grows. Meanwhile, the love that brought two people together gets pushed to the background.

When a child has ADD/ADHD, there may seem to be endless frustrations and challenges, and two very angry and tired parents make up a formula for disaster. If you are a stay-at-home parent, you may feel as if you are doing more than your share of the child-rearing work, especially if the other parent gets to "escape" to work and you don't. You may shut down and close up all communication lines, hoping that your spouse notices your pain. You may grow resentful and feel alone when he or she doesn't. And finally, you may settle for a boring, lukewarm, or mechanical relationship, sacrificing yourself and your relationship to make sure your child gets all the attention he or she needs. You may not be aware that your significant other feels the exact things that you do. Realize that the other parent could and should be a readily available source of support for you. After all, who is there in the world who understands your parental frustrations better than the person who is committed to raising the same child? Too often, however, couples take their frustrations out on each other when they should be leaning on each other for strength.

One of the best things you can do for your child and for your entire family is to make an honest effort to reconnect with your significant other and to reaffirm your love and support for each other. Whether you do this on your own or with the help of a church pastor, a therapist, or a marital counselor, it's a sine qua non of the total ADD and ADHD cure. If you, as parents, are fully supportive of each other through difficult situations and stand united and committed to the work of conquering the symptoms of ADD/ADHD with good food, good fitness, and much love and support, your children will be less inclined to act out and more willing to cooperate. In addition to doing maintenance on your relationship, you'll also want to reconnect with friends whom you've lost track of. As much as you may love your significant other, there will be times when you'll need a break from the frustrations of home life for brief periods of time, and one of the most loving things a parent can do is to take over the child-rearing duties for the day and give the other parent a day off. Going out with friends can be a good way to remind yourself to have fun and enjoy life. There's no shame in taking some time to restore yourself once in a while.

Two-Career Families

Having two parents in a family who work can present certain complications. The great temptation for both parents may be to come home and immediately begin making a display of their exhaustion so that the other feels obligated to take a larger chunk of the child-care duties. You may start scorekeeping—counting how many times you deal with a situation and contrasting this with the number of times the other parent has taken the initiative to handle a situation. Done often enough over a number of days, it becomes an unhealthy pattern in which the "chore" aspect of parenting becomes the main focus, while the joys are forgotten and lost.

Here again, your significant other needs to be your greatest source of support, and this can't happen if you each are secretly resentful or hurt. Open up communication lines and keep talking until you feel that everything is out in the open and you understand each other. A career is time-consuming and important, and you don't have to give it up entirely for the sake of your family or your relationship or marriage. However, you cannot expect your significant other to pick up the slack, and he or she cannot expect the same from you when your child is best served by attention from both of you. When both parents are truly doing their best to juggle work life with a family life that is complicated by ADD/ADHD, it may become necessary to seek support and assistance from outside sources. These options are discussed next, and they are also exactly what many single parents of ADD/ADHD children need to give their children all the care they can while also feeling relaxed, fulfilled, and happy themselves.

Single Parents

For the single parent with an ADD/ADHD-affected child, the key to staying happy and avoiding feeling overwhelmed is figuring out and taking advantage of all sources of support. People facing parenthood as couples know how hard it is and often reflect with wonder on how anyone can ever do it alone. A savvy single parent, however, has long since realized that you actually *can't* do it all alone. You need to find and accept help where you can.

If you are a single parent, start by seeking support from the school or the day care, which has a responsibility for your child's development. Guidance counselors can usually connect you to other parents facing the same problems. You can consult with these people for advice and resources, share your stories and tips, and generally support one another. Guidance counselors are usually also well informed about charitable organizations or municipal agencies that might be able to provide assistance in the way of advice and counseling.

For children who are not yet in grade school, churches, synagogues, and community groups can be vital sources of help. Do some research on the Internet for specialized playgroups, day-care centers, camps, and advocacy organizations in your area. If you find that your community doesn't offer this type of help, consider creating a group yourself. After all, ADD/ADHD affects a shockingly large portion of the population, as we know by now, and it's likely that people close at hand are facing many of the same problems. It's easier to find them than you would suspect, and they're just as happy to explore options that will make your lives easier. Above all, be concerned and attentive, but do not allow yourself to be overwhelmed by the frustrations you face in caring for a child with ADD/ADHD. Give yourself some time and some space when it is necessary and take advantage of the people and sources of love and help available to you. You and your family will be best served if you remain happy and healthy.

Seeking Outside Help

That you are exploring alternative methods to ease the symptoms of your child's ADD/ADHD and taking part in a cure already demonstrates that you are looking for help and are exploring some great options. A book, however, will only do so much in helping you to deal with the complexities of your family's situation. To address the finer details of your family's struggles, you may need to seek professional help.

Various professionals and the ways in which they can help your family have been discussed throughout this book—from psychologists to therapists to education professionals and coaches. There is no shortage of people to provide support; many times all you have to do is reach out to them. The appendix of this book offers some excellent resources and is a great place to start.

If you can detect in your other children any signs of depression and withdrawal, you'll want to find a therapist whom they can open up to. Your children may have difficulty talking about their feelings to you because they love you and don't want to worry you or hurt you. Also, please do not neglect your own happiness and emotional needs. If you find yourself struggling with self-doubt, feelings of inadequacy, feelings of neglect, anxiety, or depression, consider seeing a psychologist or a therapist who is specially trained to show you how you can be happy again. When you're happy, rested, and calm, your family as a whole has a better chance of being all these things, too.

Take great care of your children and take great care of yourself. Quite frankly, most families are eating a diet filled with sugar, artificial flavors and colors, and dairy. Not you and your family! You've changed all that. You've created a solid foundation for defeating your child's behavioral disorder. And you've made your entire family healthier while you did it. You're taking time for exercise and play. You're giving your family some of the greatest gifts you can offer. You're decreasing stress and anxiety. By changing nutrition, exercise patterns, and more, you're supporting every single family member. If you're doing your best to love and support all your family members, and enjoying the love you get in return, then you have everything you need to cure a lot of things—not just ADD/ADHD. Live well, enjoy life, and set your children up to do the same, every day.

You've done it. Keep going. It's worth it.

RESOURCES

Educational Publishers

American Guidance Services (AGS)
4201 Woodland Road
P.O. Box 90
Circle Pines, MN 55014-1796

Developmental Learning Materials (DLM)
One DLM Park
Allen, TX 75002-1302

Free Spirit Publishing, Inc.
400 First Avenue, North, Suite 616
Minneapolis, MN 55401-1724

Books

Diet for a New America by John Robbins

Fast Food Nation: The Dark Side of the All-American Meal by Eric Schlosser

I Eat at Mommy's by Anna E. Bradley-McBeth et al.

The New Laurel's Kitchen: A Handbook for Vegetarian Cookery and Nutrition by Laurel Robertson, Brian Ruppenthal, and Carol L. Flinders

Prescription for Nutritional Healing: A Practical A–Z Reference to Drug-Free Remedies Using Vitamins, Minerals, Herbs, and Food Supplements, 3rd edition, by Phyllis Balch and James Balch

Smart Medicine for a Healthier Child: A Practical A-to-Z Reference to Natural and Conventional Treatments for Infants and Children, 2nd edition, by Janet Zand et al.

Magazines and Newsletters

ATTENTION (magazine)
CH.A.D.D. National Headquarters
499 Northwest 70th Avenue, Suite 308
Plantation, FL 33317
305-587-3700
www.CHADD.org

Attention Please (Newsletter for children with attention deficit disorder)
2106 3rd Avenue North
Seattle, WA 98109

BRAKES: The Interactive Newsletter for Kids with ADHD
Magination Press
19 Union Square West
New York, NY 10003
800-825-3089

Organizations/Support Groups

American Academy of Pediatrics
141 Northwest Point Boulevard
Elk Grove Village, IL 60007
847-434-4000
www.aap.org

American Speech-Language-Hearing Association (ASHS)
10801 Rockville Pike
Rockville, MD 20849-1725
301-897-5700

Attention Deficit Disorder Association
1788 Second Street, Suite 200
Highland Park, IL 60035
847-432-ADDA
www.add.org

Children and Adults with Attention Deficit Hyperactivity Disorder
  (CHADD)
8181 Professional Place, Suite 201
Landover, MD 20785
800-233-4050
www.chadd.org

ERIC Clearinghouse on Handicapped and Gifted Children
Council for Exceptional Children (CEC)
1920 Association Drive
Reston, VA 22091-1589
800-438-8841

National Association for Gifted Children
1155 15th Street NW, Suite 1002
Washington, DC 20005
202-785-4286

Parent Advocacy Coalition for Educational Rights (PACER)
4826 Chicago Avenue, South
Minneapolis, MN 55417
612-827-2966

Web Resources

Alternatives to Dairy Products
www.notmilk.com/altmilk.html

Cereals Information Sheet
www.vegsoc.org/info/cereals.html

Go Dairy Free
www.godairyfree.org

Hidden Animal Ingredients
www.cyberparent.com/eat/hiddenanimalsinfood.htm

How to Know If You're Lactose Intolerant
www.lalecheleague.org/ba/Nov98.html

Nuts and Seeds Information Sheet
www.vegsoc.org/info/nutsseeds.html

Nutrients for Vegetarians and Vegans
www.cyberparent.com/eat/nutrientsvegan.htm

The Vegetarian Resource Group
www.vrg.org

Universities That Provide Special Educational Opportunities for Young Adults with ADHD

American International College (MA)
Barat College of DePaul University (IL)
College of Mount St. Joseph (OH)
Beacon College (FL)
Bernau College (GA)
Chicago State University (IL)
Curry College (MA)
DePaul University (IL)
East Tennessee State University (TN)
Farleigh Dickinson University (NJ)
Finlandia University (MI)
Illinois State University (IL)
Limestone College (NC)
Lynn University (FL)
Marshall University (WV)
Southern Illinois University (IL)
Texas Tech University (TX)
University of Arizona (AZ)
University of Colorado at Boulder (CO)

University of Denver (CO)
University of Illinois (IL)
University of the Ozarks (AR)
University of Wisconsin at Whitewater (WI)
West Virginia Wesleyan College (WV)
Western Carolina University (NC)

INDEX